LEADING UP, DOWN AND ACROSS

LEADING UP, DOWN AND ACROSS

BECOME A BETTER LEADER TODAY!

Jochen Hekker

Published by: LiDRS in control BV
Editor: Nienke van Oeveren (Book editing)
Cover design and in-text design: Adept Vormgeving
Photographs: Dutch Ministry of Defense
Translation: Dakota Language Services

First edition
Copyright @ 2014, Jochen Hekker
Original title: Leiders!
ISBN: 978-90-822429-1-1
Nur: 808

The members are not to request me, merely to order me and if I were ordered to carry the nation's flag on but a single vessel, I will sail out to sea and there, entrusted with the members' flag, I shall risk life and limb***

Michiel Adriaenszoon de Ruyter, 17th Century Dutch Admiral
(24 March 1607 - 29 April 1676)

*** Loosely translated from a reaction by De Ruyter to a
member of the States General, who questioned his courage.

For Max, Finn and Sem ....

TABLE OF CONTENTS

INTRODUCTION

Many years ago, I crossed the threshold of the 'Royal Netherlands Naval College', to begin a career full of adventure and challenges. I actually had no idea what lay ahead of me. There were wonderful stories in a colorful brochure and a commercial oozing adventure, but I was clueless about what would cross my path. I certainly wasn't aware that the organization would try to prep me to become a commanding officer. I wasn't aware that I was going to face different types of leaders all around me. Every two to three years would bring a new position, new colleagues, new responsibilities and, in particular, new challenges.

This book is about my experiences: a growth process towards the unattainable objective of 'perfect' leadership, obviously not without some reserve. However, my reality may also contribute to your views of leadership. You learn how to lead by experience and by listening, reading, studying and observing. In the end, you will choose the elements that you think may be of interest for the way you lead.

LEARNING FROM GOOD AND BAD LEADERSHIP
There is a lot of literature available on leadership, but which of the many books on the topic do you still use today and which model can you still reproduce? Here lies the benefit of this book. This is a book you are going to use! Appealing stories and a leadership model that is easy to apply will foster your growth as a leader. Not everyone has the opportunity to experience leadership in an organization like the Ministry of Defense. An organization with its own culture, people and circumstances that are not branded as 'ordinary'; an organization that pours a great deal of time and effort into training its leaders, yet despite all its endeavors, still doesn't succeed in delivering only good leaders. Even within an organization like the Ministry of Defense, leadership is subject to change. Even there, leadership based on rank or position is a thing of the past. Unfortunately, this change is not self-evident for everyone.

In this book, I will provide examples of good and bad leadership. The stories will present leadership features that are also within you. By making these features transparent and grouping them creatively, it will allow you to make a simple assessment of yourself, but also of others in their role as leaders. It will make you aware of your strong and weak features and you will be able to work on developing your own leadership skills.

However, there are many theoretical models, practical tips and scores of examples and questionnaires out there to help determine your leadership style. You can get the most peculiar labels pinned on you: tiger, dolphin, rabbit, thinker, doer, dictator, servant, coach, narcissist and many others. For every variable in leadership, a name has been invented and for every idea out there, there is a graph or theory that is difficult to decipher.

All these difficult to understand theories and the many fancy labels are precisely what I have tried to avoid when writing 'Leading up, down and across'. You can subject leadership to thousands of studies, but everyone experiences it differently and every leader will base his or her style of leadership on experiences, knowledge, character and personality. A practically applicable leadership model or a frantic attempt to frame a leadership style will require a flexible point of departure. After all, there are scores of variables that determine which elements of leadership are required in a certain situation. This is precisely where 'Leading up, down and across' has a lot to offer you.

THE STRUCTURE OF THE BOOK
This book consists of two parts. I call the first part 'The Story', where I describe my experiences in a predominantly maritime and military environment. The second part, 'The Theory', presents a theoretical framework, resulting in a flexible and easy-to-use leadership model.

Sharing my experiences in Part One provides you with a broader frame of reference for leadership. Each story emphasizes leadership elements that serve as building blocks for the ultimate leadership model.

Figure 1: Possible building blocks of leadership

Stories for example about basic military training, sailing on board a marine frigate, deployments to Afghanistan and sometimes general lessons in leadership, make these stories not only meaningful for leaders within the Ministry of Defense, but for those outside the military as well. In fact, you will probably be surprised to note the many similarities between leadership experiences inside and outside of the Ministry of Defense. In particular, the emphatic way of presenting the different leadership styles gives rise to an improved and broadened frame of reference. Still, not every building block will seem equally relevant for each individual model. Clustering and selecting building blocks takes place in the second part of the book.

In the theoretical second part, I use the building blocks to shape the model; a model you can use easily and flexibly to assess and improve your leadership style. The model consists of universal, 'critical' characteristics of leadership that are important to you, regardless of the organization for which you work, the number of people you manage or the circumstances in which you find yourself. This is the LiDRS model.[1] With this model, you will be able to navigate on the ideal characteristics of leadership. Not only will you have the opportunity to assess yourself and others, the model also provides the possibility to request feedback about the way you function as a leader. Finally, there are several examples of others who have served as leaders under similar circumstances. This model will allow you to see how they applied their skills in those situations. In order to implement the model, you will need to use the online LiDRS model (www.lidrs.eu).

---

[1] LiDRS is an organisation active in leadership training courses. The name is an abbreviation of Leadership Development, Research and Support.

THE RIGHT SETTINGS

By the end of this book, you will not only have expanded your frame of reference about leadership through many stories supported by practical tips, but you will also know which simple adjustments to make, in order to master your style of leadership. However, for this book the type of leader you are does not matter, nor does the extent of your experience. The right to lead is something you earn by discovering the best use of the model for your circumstances. The experienced, charismatic leader will probably need to make far fewer adjustments to the model than will the new, less experienced leader. It makes no difference how many adjustments you need to make, as long as you thoroughly assess the management situation and the persons whom you manage.

In this book, no distinction is made between male and female managers. For convenience, I have elected to label the leader in this book as male. This is why the leader in this book is referred to as 'he'. Obviously, this may just as well be read as 'she'.

PART I

THE STORY

1. RAGGING

Knowledge is power, character goes beyond.
- Motto of the Royal Netherlands Naval Institute

Even years later, almost every naval cadet speaks highly of the Corps Introduction Period, the period in which future officers are 'shown the ropes'. Obviously, the program has changed here and there over the years, but the essence remains the same. As future officers of the Royal Navy, the cadets are playfully taught some of the customs that may be of use to them later in life. During the 1997 introduction period, the training program began with 120 persons, but this number quickly shrank to far below 100. There were different reasons for this, of course: physical complaints, homesickness, social isolation, an overly authoritarian environment, childish ragging and many more. However, when looking back on the period of 'ragging', be it in the military, as a student or in some other community, many of its elements serve a specific purpose, which may be of benefit to you later on as a leader.

A NEW CHALLENGE
'*Name?*' the lady behind the table asked me. I was in a large hall of the main building of the 'Royal Netherlands Naval College'. The place was just oozing maritime nostalgia. The high walls were draped with impressive paintings of naval battles and probably some world famous naval heroes as well. I just didn't know them yet. The oak parquet floor was a shiny dark brown.

Over the large wooden entrance doors of the hall, a motto read: '*Knowledge is power - character goes beyond.*'
Wasn't I here for a five-year university education? How, I wondered, could this motto be displayed here so prominently, in an environment of learning? I would soon find out, however, that knowledge is indeed power, but knowledge alone will not get you very far. Looking around

19

me some more, it seemed quite possible that very little had changed in this hall over the past two hundred years.

'Hekker, madam,' I said politely. I was impressed with the entourage. Several cadets were walking around, all of them smartly dressed in uniforms with rank insignia, shiny emblems and more prints that I wasn't familiar with, but which, in any case, indicated they must have accomplished something. The uniform was a dark blue suit with red details on the collar and of course, they wore smartly fastened black ties and shiny black shoes. Yes, the cadets looked very sharp indeed.

The woman at the table pushed a paper under my nose. *'Sign here, here and there,'* she said, while leafing through an expensive-looking stack of papers. At the time, I didn't realize that I was committing to the Navy for thirteen years. Even if I had known this, I would have given my signature without hesitation. I signed the various copies, one of which was handed back to me. I stuck my copy into my backpack. *'Well, Mister Hekker. Welcome! Your personal number is 062579. You can move on to one of the next tables for further instructions. Good luck in your naval career.'* Over the next ninety minutes, I was sent from one table to another. Each time, I had to state my name, sign papers and fill in my personal information. At the end, having visited all of the tables, I hung my backpack over my shoulder again and walked in the direction of a cluster of armchairs by a small table, in a corner of the large room. I joined some people of my own age there, all of whom were anxiously awaiting what would follow, just as I was. I looked at them, surprised by all the different characters who had decided to follow the same path, passing the same tables. There was Marc from Heerlen, long hair, worn Metallica T-shirt and the indisputable Southern accent; Bastiaan from Arnhem, neat pants, boat shoes, Ralph Lauren polo shirt, blond hair, weighing a solid 220 pounds; Freek from Amsterdam, graduated from the Maritime Academy, dressed in student attire and now on the threshold of a naval career; Vincent from Den Helder, son of a naval officer, smartly dressed, like Bastiaan, he was the only one who looked as if he had been walking around here for years; Ivo, given to laughter, the pretty boy from the eastern part of the country; Alrik from The Hague, one black eye from playing rugby and a nice shiny flowery shirt, a genuine The Hague accent and a big golden chain around his neck. Over 100 young people had come together in this old traditional hall to embark on an adventure together - one that for many would prove to be the wrong choice.

The main building of the Royal Netherlands Naval College

IN THE NEW

'*Listen up!*' one of the naval cadets shouted through the hall. I turned around and in the middle of the grand room and saw a cadet with a stack of papers in his hands. '*The people whom I call next will follow second-year Jansen.*' Second-year Jansen stood before the big, heavy wooden doors. The moment his name was called, he straightened his legs, snapping together the heels of his recently shined shoes. He stretched his back, the arms straight along his body and he looked stoutly ahead. Aalbers, Aarts, Anders, a list of names was called out, up to Hekker. So there I went, in the first group, following 'second-year Jansen'. Outside the hall, we were positioned in a line next to each other. From the look on his face, I gathered that this was not done quickly enough to suit second-year Jansen, but he kept his comments to himself. '*Good afternoon everyone, my name is second-year Jansen. Here's what we will do this afternoon.*' He read off a list of activities, starting with a haircut, and I asked myself how we would ever be able to pull all that off in one afternoon. When I saw the first person getting out of the barber's chair after less than sixty seconds, however, I knew that my frame of reference was rather off the mark. It took a mere sixty seconds to turn a bunch of full, flowing manes into short buzz cuts, a crop that would look good in a bad prison movie. The result was not much better for the women: clipped straight, high above their shoulders. Luckily, my hair was already short to begin with, so my looks did not undergo too drastic a transformation in sixty seconds. It was clear that this was an age-old 'enrollment' procedure. In no time, we had completed all of the activities and were walking around in peculiar, ugly, blue fatigues, on our way to our sleeping quarters.

The dormitory was a large hall, measuring sixty-five by one-hundred and sixty five feet, filled with bunk beds and lockers. The ceiling was at least twenty feet high and fitted with big fluorescent tube casings. The space was divided across its entire width, by a number of partitions that were as high as the bunk beds, to form ten corridors with bunk beds on both sides and lockers at the head and foot of the beds. One locker was for the person sleeping on the top bed and the other was for the person on the bottom bed. At the north side of the dormitory, there were huge windows, reaching almost up to the ceiling. On the southern end, there was a big blank wall, with an opening in the middle, serving as the entrance to what was referred to as the 'free republic', which for the new cadets was nothing more than a room to wash up in. Along the walls, there were washbasins and taped up mirrors. As it turned out, the mirrors had been taped up especially for the introduction period. Over 100 men would be sharing the 30 washbasins in there. *'Find your own bunk, get your toiletries out of your bag and then return to me. You have one minute!'* Jansen shouted.

And so we wandered around like headless chickens, looking for our names on the small stacks of things arranged on the beds. I found my name on a bed in the middle of the dorm. The label read: 'Baroe Hek-ker'. Baroe, baroe? I wondered what in heaven's name the word 'baroe' meant. I fished my toiletry bag and a book to read out of my backpack and walked over to second-year Jansen. After a while, the group was complete again and everybody had found their beds. I could tell Jansen wasn't too pleased and he looked frustrated. *'Well, well, that took you long enough.'* he said to the group. Then he led the way to the attic, where we could store our stuff. *'Your belongings will remain under lock and key until further notice.'* Jansen said. *'Anything you may need will be provided by the State.'* So there we were, without our personal belongings, shaved heads and not knowing what lay ahead, all of us looking at second-year Jansen.

In the days that followed, we spent most of our time waiting. Standing behind our bunk beds, we were obliged to read the book about the Naval Cadet Corps: the code of conduct, the history of the corps, but also the cadet corps hymn and the first and sixth verses of the Dutch national anthem, *The Wilhelmus.* In between studying, we were given all sorts of items that would have easily allowed us to participate in the 1944 invasion of Normandy, or so I thought. It wasn't just the amount of stuff we were given, but also the state everything was in. Practical? Maybe so, but certainly not comfortable. The rucksack was filled with a smelly sleeping bag, mess-kit, rain poncho, mat, tent, tent pegs, undershirts, more blue fatigues, canteen and all sorts of small items that I had no idea what to do with. A couple of days later, over 120 men were packed up and ready, waiting on a boat to take us to the Dutch Wadden island of Texel, for our first practical introduction to the military world.

DEALING WITH INSECURITIES
As a freshman, a beginner or *baroe* (rookie), you step into a new world, making yourself vulnerable. You are left at the mercy of a senior and all of his whims. Coming from the secure environment of your home, where your parents serve as a safety net, you suddenly have to do it all yourself, starting from the bottom of the hierarchical ladder. There is but one goal, of course, to become a member and eventually to get off the bottom step of this ladder, to achieve 'fame' and 'prestige' and maybe even a 'hero's status' inside your own little crew. You are expected to apply a great deal of social skill in order to give shape to your role. At the time, all you think is, 'What am I doing here and how long is this going to take?' However, looking back, you won't be able to remember the bad times very well. You will put them in perspective, while the time factor also assumes different dimensions. *'Ah well, how long did I really spend working on that task?'*

Dealing with insecurities will ensure that you put things in perspective. You will not be put down easily when things don't go according to plan. There will be plenty of occasions in life when you will not be able to influence matters. Then there is also your insecurity about your role in a new group. As humans, we aim to evaluate our own opinions and experiences. If we make wrong assessments in this regard, we won't be able to collect rewards or avoid punishment.[2] In familiar surroundings,

---

[2] J. Nuttin; V. Hoorens - *Sociale beïnvloeding; toetsbaar leren over gedrag*; about social influencing and verifiable learning about behaviour, Leuven University Press, 2008

your opinion and experience were acknowledged all the time. Your position within the group was a given: among classmates, at the sports club, but also within your circle of friends. From the moment when I first set foot in that hall at the Royal Netherlands Naval College and made the acquaintance of my fellow new students, there was insecurity about my position in the group and whether my own perception of my opinion and skills was correct. The more you are faced with such situations, the easier it will be to deal with them and the more self-assured you become. Everyone faces some degree of insecurity each day.

Dealing with insecurities is relevant for everyone. It may be insecurity over being stuck in a queue or about that one appointment, the location and time of which you can't exactly remember. You may be insecure about the first visit to a new client, or perhaps the first meeting with your new employer. What is important in situations like this is that you manage to put it all into perspective. If you are certain that you cannot exert any influence on it, it will be better for you to find the calm within yourself, which will, in any case, help you make the right decisions. The insecurity about your role in a group or in a new environment primarily has to do with your social characteristics. After all, the other people are just as interested in you, as you are in them. In addition, it's just as well to know people have already formed an opinion of you in advance, as that will then be one thing about which you won't need to worry.[3]

> **Building blocks of leadership:**
> *Sense of perspective, self-assured*

---

[3] T. IJzermans; L. Eckhardt - *Het woord is nu aan u!; onstpannen spreken in het openbaar*; about relaxed public speaking, Thema publishing company; 2009

THE RHYTHM SENSE OF A TAWNY OWL

There we were, on the island of Texel. All around me there were bald heads, and ladies who looked uncomfortable with the short haircuts, blue fatigues and sheep that covered the Texel landscape. The backpack contributed to the uncomfortable feeling. I wondered how long I would have to carry the horrible thing around. The straps felt like they were actually carving their way into the flesh of my shoulders. Maybe someone was secretly hanging on to it, but unfortunately, it really was just gravity at work. I looked around and noticed everybody was just standing around, not really knowing what to do. I decided to enjoy the wonderful August sun on Texel a bit and not think too much about the backpack.

My moment of peace was short-lived, though. *'Listen up!'* a marine in a green uniform yelled. I already knew the marines were the Navy's 'top athletes' and this one looked every bit the part. *'There are lists at the back of this bus, dividing you into groups. I want the leaders of each group with me in five minutes. Execute!'* he roared across the Texel landscape. Just like that, 120 men scrambled towards the bus, which was covered in lists. The top of each list read 'platoon' with a number, followed by a couple of names. *'Platoon 6, Amsterdam, Bakker, Schilder, Verschuren, Aalbers, Hekker'* I quickly read. In the end, 120 men were divided into ten platoons of twelve men each. After several minutes Amsterdam, our platoon leader, who had been appointed by our commanders, returned with a map of Texel. The route marked on it appeared to direct us to a huge barracks compound. We were also given a surprise package in the form of a steel chain, twenty-three feet in length, weighing about 175 pounds, which we had to carry along with us. Oh, and if we would please hurry up, there was a time limit on this assignment. Twelve men stood in a circle around the chain, wondering how in the world they were going to pull this off. I turned and saw some other groups looking just as stunned as we did and up ahead, the first group was already underway across the bicycle path, away from the harbor, towards the Texel no man's land. Minutes later, platoon six had formed a long winding row and we set off in search of the barracks, walking along the trail with the huge chain on our shoulders, which we rested on the backpacks that were already so heavy on their own. One advantage of the chain was that it shifted your attention away from the straps of the rucksack cutting into your shoulders. This was one heavy chain! At least every eighty feet I could hear somebody utter *'damn!'*

or '*ouch*!' immediately followed by another voice saying '*sorry.*' We were stepping on each other's heels all the time, which could be pretty painful, considering the fact that we wore new, rigid army boots that had not been broken in yet.

Actually it was one huge miserable affair. I don't know what I hated most: the chain, the boots, my backpack, or by this time, the sun. I could feel my heart rate rising quite a bit and cursed at the August sun. The skin on my neck was burning and with the weight of the load we had to carry, the effort made to coordinate the cadence and the pace at which we were moving, the sweat was now running down my back. Marc was walking behind me and I noticed that at least he had a sense of rhythm and he was able to follow my cadence reasonably well. The number of times my heels were stepped on was minimal. Luckily, I managed to also keep the heels of the man in front of me fairly intact. Others in the group were not as fortunate. The one lady in our company turned out to have poor motor skills. After about a ten-minute hike, we stopped by the side of the bicycle path. I looked around and I could just see the Texel boat departing for Den Helder. What a setback this was, we had covered maybe just half a mile or so. Our one female platoon member was democratically removed from the group of chain bearers. The entire group was fed up with her continuous moaning already and we had only been on Texel for an hour. Amsterdam had the lead and he looked at the route we had been given. He analyzed the possibilities together with us and rearranged the group of chain bearers. Four and a half hours later, we reached the barracks compound. We'd made it.

PERSEVERANCE

Here we were, away from the protection of our parents, away from our usual Saturday at the local sports club. Instead, we were on Texel, carrying a heavy chain draped over our shoulders. Suddenly we were expected to put in an impossible physical effort. At least we thought it was impossible, until now. As it turns out, however, we were capable of a lot more than we would have thought. These were physically draining tours across the island, in the company of a platoon, the members of which included our beloved steel chain that took ages to complete. When we arrived, we threw the chain off our shoulders, removed the heavy helmets from our heads and dropped onto the grass, totally exhausted. Spent, broken, and demolished, but we made it. It's moments like this when you think: How long will this go on? If only I were back home, especially on a nice summer's day like this one, on my friends' patio, enjoying the sun. Wearing shorts and sandals and maybe drinking a nice cold beer, but instead you hear '*GET UP!*' after just a couple of minutes rest. '*You still don't get it,*' one of the supervisors shouted. '*It took you four and a half hours to get here! This was planned for two hours! So how long have I been waiting? Exactly! Much too long! Everybody up! The group leaders have all received a new route and you will start your new march NOW!*' At such a moment, something inside you just snaps. For a split second you wonder whether you've gone crazy. You're broken, but you also don't want to give in. You get up, tie your shoes again, pick up your backpack and help your buddies get their stuff ready. When you walk away a little later with a smaller group and you see a number of people have just given up, you realize that the real leaders are the ones who are still walking. Of course there are special cases, cases of real physical discomfort, but you'd be surprised to find out how much your body can take, as much as you want to. These are the obstacles you must face from time to time. You have to know where your limits lie as a human being, but also as a leader. You start walking again.

Future naval officers suffering on Texel.

I clearly remember my father coming home one day and asking me if I wanted to practice martial arts. Our neighbor owned a gym where he taught 'Kenpo', a Chinese form of martial arts. So there I went, at seven years of age. Every Sunday, I would hitch a ride with our neighbor to Kenpo class. Over thirty adult men and one skinny little kid. The men all just loved it and so I kept it up, year in, year out, riding with our neighbor every Sunday morning. I developed a real taste for martial arts and in my teens I also took up Kyokushinkai karate, a full contact style of sport fighting, three times a week on top of the hours spent on Kenpo.

What a complete culture shock my first karate class was. Until then, every Sunday morning, I would get to the Kenpo gym, chat with people first, then bow to the instructor and work on my fitness for an hour, with some more chatting in between exercises. It was all nice and relaxed. In the second hour we would work on Kenpo fighting techniques. At Kenpo, people would regularly show up late, change clothes, mumble 'Morning' and join the session.

Then came my first karate class. I went into the locker room and cheerfully said 'Hello' to everybody there. Those who came in after me just let out a powerful 'Ush', which was greeted by everybody with a similar 'Ush!' Later, I learned that 'Ush' has a very broad meaning. It serves as a greeting, but it can also mean that something has been understood or any number of other things. There wasn't much talking in the locker room, everybody was busy straightening their uniforms and tying belts. The men would throw punches in the air, creating a snappy, whipping sound with the sleeves of their uniforms. Afterwards they would head for the door to the gym. The people in the gym were greeted with a powerful '*Ush!*' and at the same time, there was that whipping sound from the sleeves again, a noise that sounded like '*Tak!*' caused by the swift movement of the arms. 'Ush' was pronounced powerfully, while the arms were crossed before the face and then whipped downward. At the start of the session, everyone would assume the lotus position in front of the instructors. Whenever they were asked if something was clear, the room would call out in unison: 'Ush!'

There was no talking, only exercising; everything was 'Ush,' all in proper karate position, throughout the session. If someone came in late, he would greet the room, 'Ush.' However, don't expect this person to be allowed to just join in. He would assume the lotus position; face the wall with a straight back and his fists in his sides, waiting for the instructor to get him. This could sometimes take longer than half a session, even if you came in just three minutes late.

Sparring sessions, the actual fighting was done without shin protection or gloves. There obviously is a reason why Kyokushinkai refers to the ultimate truth. It's a tough discipline in a tough fighting sport. I absolutely loved it! I had learned how to defend myself fairly well through the years, practicing Kenpo, but here you were taught how to actually 'fight'. Low kicks, persevere and fight hard! Even when you think you can't go on, you put up your fists and straighten your back, 'Ush' and go! By standing straight, you emanate aggressiveness and a will to win, providing you with a psychological advantage over your opponent. A little character goes a long way. This was when I first discovered that your body can take a lot more abuse than you think. Often it is your mind that betrays you. During these intense Kyokushinkai sessions the meaning of discipline and perseverance became clear to me, but I especially learned how to push through boundaries. I am convinced that these sessions gave me more than merely the means to defend myself. Giving up is a choice you make yourself.

So when we were walking around with that chain on our shoulders, how easy would it have been to call it quits on this summer's day? However, a leader soldiers on. A leader rises and takes the initiative. When everybody is having a hard time, he will appeal to the group's sense of belonging. He will appoint himself coach and will be able to motivate people. He will disregard his own misery and focus on those who suffer, with a view to the ultimate goal of finishing as a team.

> **Building blocks of leadership:**
> *Resilience, Charisma*

BEARER OF BAD NEWS

The barracks, our new home base, had little to offer the 120 rookies. There were ten dome tents on a stretch of grass, positioned in a wide circle. Each platoon had its own dome tent and each tent had twelve green stretchers. This was our bedroom and dining room for the time being. It was quite clear that we would not be bathing in opulence while we were there. I dropped my dreadful rucksack next to a stretcher and plopped down on it.

'Hekker!!' I heard my name being called from across the field. I heaved a deep sigh. 'Now what?' Both my feet and my head clearly preferred that I not get up. I dragged myself out of the tent and saw one of the marines on the other side of the field beckoning me. Since everything around the encampment had to be done running, I sprinted to the man in green. *'Hekker, as of now, you will be our class elder,'* the marine said, and then without pausing for so much as a single breath he ordered me to get the entire group, all ten platoons, 120 men, on their feet again. Before I was able to ask what 'class elder' meant, let alone inquire further about the order, the man in green had disappeared. This is how, in the first week, I became the contact person for both the instructors of this 'military training' as well as for my classmates. In fact, I became the bearer of bad news. The instructors would use me to communicate the most dreadful tasks to the group, but I was also the one to express the displeasure of the group to the instructors. Lists of chores, distribution of tasks, bringing bad news to individual members and all other matters that required some degree of finesse. However, most of the time, I would trot across the bicycle paths of Texel in the company of Platoon 6 and a large chain, asking myself how much longer we would have to endure this agony. As it turned out, it would be three weeks. Three weeks full of morning exercises, marching, endurance, carrying the chain, sleeping in tents, few showers, more morning exercises, deadlines, impossible deadlines, irritations, frustrations, and hunger... Slowly, but surely, the 120 individuals were transformed into a tight military community, which would eventually be referred to as the 'Class of '97'. After three weeks, we saw the Texel boat coming in from Den Helder. There we were, ten platoons in military position. The boots had been broken in smoothly and nobody seemed to notice the rucksacks they were carrying over their shoulders anymore. The blue cap we had received on our first day had been replaced by a brand-new beret with an anchor. We had really survived a lot. Or so we thought, perhaps a bit naively...

TEAMWORK

One hundred and twenty individuals took their first steps in the Royal Netherlands Naval College, in the late summer of 1997. Eventually, these individuals were molded into a team. After all, you don't carry around a heavy chain all by yourself. You are dependent on each other and you must make use of each other's qualities. Teamwork. A leader knows how to bring out everyone's strengths and knows how to use this strength together. He is capable of creating a team out of a group of individuals. During that first hike with the chain across the island of Texel, people were cursing at each other within a couple of minutes. The chain was too heavy, the boots hurt, people would constantly step on the heels of those in front of them. Irritations, frustrations. The Platoon leader at the time, dealt with it perfectly. The woman with the poor motor skills was removed from the company carrying the chain. She was positioned on the side, to talk to everyone and entertain the group with fun stories. The group leader also knew how to put things into perspective at the right time. Just when you would start thinking about your aching heels, the rucksack chafing against your shoulders, the pressure from the heavy chain and the blistering sun burning your head, the group leader managed to bring it all back to reality with a single remark. *'Men, it's a good thing the sun is shining, imagine if it were raining right now. That would've been awful.'* or *'We're lucky, we don't have to do this wearing slippers.'*

Why is it so important for a leader to be able to create a team out of a group of individuals? The answer is easy; individuals are capable of less and they know less than a well-oiled team working together, with their knowledge and capabilities combined. The leader also needs to show that he is a good judge of character and that he is able to utilize everyone's best qualities, making the best interests of the team clear. [4] The leader needs to be able to make the objective of the team clear. The atmosphere of a team is important. The individuals must be prepared to put their best foot forward through an intrinsic motivation. The leader serves as a catalyst here.

---

[4] A.H. Bell; D.M. Smith - *Learning Team Skills; Pearson Education* 2003

The future naval cadets engaging in a team effort.

WHAT A PERFORMANCE

Proud as peacocks, the class of '97 marched in a column off the Texel boat in Den Helder and off the quay, onto the premises of the Royal Netherlands Naval College. To the left and right stood the civilian staff, officers and naval cadets, waiting for us and greeting us with applause. What a performance we put in, three 'whole weeks' on Texel. We sang the marching hymn even louder, eyes straight ahead, brand-new berets pulled tight over our heads. Those who were suffering from minor aches and pains weren't bothered by them at that moment. Left, right, left, right, arms stretched out, straight and forward, with a fixed gaze. We already knew that we'd made an amazing showing on Texel, but this was now confirmed by real soldiers. Unfortunately, I realized then and there, that it actually wasn't all that amazing and that in the two hundred years before this, just as many boys and girls had done the same thing.

As soon as we entered the Royal Netherlands Naval College's compound, we dropped our rucksacks and sang the self-composed class of '97 song, horribly off-key, making our way back to the dormitory where we had spent so much time prior to being shipped off to Texel. Again, and for the umpteenth time, I was studying the Naval Cadets' hymn. Fortunately, not half an hour later, we were taken down to the familiar hall where I had signed the contract that first afternoon. This time, I had survived three weeks of Texel. So much had changed in such a short while.

'*Good evening,*' one of the older cadets shouted through the hall. '*My name is senior student Jacob and you are currently in the hall. This room is the meeting place for the Naval Cadet Corps. The hall is divided into three sections. One general area, one second years' area and a senior years' area. Normally, it is not permitted for a junior to enter the senior area without invitation. Since the Corps is proud of your achievements on Texel, it has been decided to arrange a nice party and make the entire room available for this. Enjoy yourselves!*' Then one of the doors to the side was opened and a couple of cadets came in with beers in hand. It was obvious that this was the entrance to the naval cadet bar. In no time, a cadet was standing in front of me, holding two beers. He stuck out his hand and introduced himself as second-year Moormans. '*Jochen,*' I said with a big smile. '*I got you a beer,*' second-year Moormans said. So for a while there, it felt as if we were having a nice chat about the time on Texel. Every now and then, someone would come up to me, only to soon disappear again. I could not help but feel that something was going on. The cadets were making too much of an effort to come across as friendly. Some of them were whispering in groups about a couple of my fellow students. Luckily, Marc, who had become my mate, was having a good time down by the bar. He was born and bred in Limburg province and he probably couldn't resist the delights of beer, because he was having a real go at it. I hoped he wouldn't drink too much, because his was the bunk above mine. After about an hour and a half, senior cadet Jacob announced that all cadets were expected to return to the bar and all future cadets should return to the dormitory. We all went to brush our teeth and got ready for a well-deserved night's sleep. I crept into bed and said goodnight to Marc above me, but he was probably sound asleep already, considering all the beers he'd downed. I mused on the day we'd had and then decided to enjoy a good night's rest. But how deceptive appearances can be…

CORPS INTRODUCTION

'*Clack, clack, clack*' All of the fluorescent lights on the ceiling went on. I woke up with a start, out of a deep sleep, not knowing where I was for a second. '*Everybody in front of the lockers!!!*' The loud voice resonated through the dormitory. I rubbed my eyes and wondered what was going on. It felt like the middle of the night to me. Everybody crawled out of bed and walked to the end of the corridor of beds, in front of the lockers. There we were, in our tight blue pajamas. Many must've been woken from mildly erotic dreams, considering the evidence that could be seen clearly through the tight blue Smurf outfits. In front of us, on a bench, there were two naval cadets from each platoon, staring straight ahead. There could not have been a bigger contrast between our appearances. They were elevated, on a bench, smartly dressed in uniforms, fit as fiddles, while we were in our pajamas on the floor, only barely awake. I presumed that something had gone wrong, because the ladies and gentlemen did not look very happy at all. The long row of benches that the cadets were standing on was broken up in the middle of the dormitory by the entrance to the large number of washbasins, the 'free republic'. There, on the floor, in between the benches with the cadets stood senior cadet Jacob. He was the one who had called for everybody to stand in front of the lockers.

'*I am disappointed,*' senior Jacob yelled. '*I am terribly disappointed in you. The reactions from the Naval Cadet Corps are as plain as day. What a pack of ill-mannered, unmotivated, arrogant dogs! Baroes, the lot of you! Baroes! Never, in the history of this magnificent institute, has such a motley crew as you, entered these premises. What happened there on Texel?*' Jacob was silent for a moment, probably needing to catch his breath after the outburst. You could hear a pin drop.

'*The flag officer in charge of officers training has therefore decided to hand you over to the Naval Cadet Corps as of this moment and to leave it to us, to try and make something out of you yet.*' Jacob continued. '*Standing in front of you is the Corps' Introduction Committee. From now on, they will determine when you eat, sleep, drink and go to the bathroom, is that clear?*' he said, as he sternly looked down the row where I was standing. '*Yeah, yeah, okay,*' some mumbled that it was understood. '*Is that clear!!*' senior cadet Jacob once again hollered through the dormitory, his red face almost turning crimson. '*Yes!*' everybody yelled in unison. '*Then I now introduce you to the chairman of*

34

the Introduction Committee, senior cadet Luter. Attention!' We assumed the position we had learned on Texel only a few days earlier. Within seconds, senior cadet Luter walked in. He entered the room with big steps. The cadets sprang into position and looked straight ahead. This must have to be a very important person, I guessed. Senior cadet Luter stood near senior cadet Jacob, at the corner of one of the benches. He looked past the rows from left to right. 'Well here we are in our blue Smurf outfits,' I thought, expecting a tirade from this senior, but the contrary proved to be the case. *'Ladies and Gentlemen.'* He briefly paused before he continued, *'I was in total disbelief when I learned of your failed performance this evening. Now I have been appointed to teach you a thing or two. I guarantee you that I will succeed. I demand maximum effort and swift improvement from you. Do not let me down!'* The way he spoke, the brief pauses he took, the penetrating look he gave everybody, ensured that the message came across. *'Fellow corps members,'* he addressed the naval cadets around him, *'do what you have to do and ensure that this disorderly bunch quickly learns the ropes of the Naval Cadet Corps, whatever it takes.'* Senior cadet Luter stepped off the bench and walked out of the dormitory, taking the same big steps. As soon as he'd left, senior cadet Jacob ordered everybody to stand at ease. I relaxed my muscles and took an easier pose. *'Everybody will now go back to bed and tomorrow we'll see what you're all made of.'* For the second time that night, I crept into bed. This time, however, my feeling of invincibility had completely disappeared and I wondered what lay ahead of us. 'Whatever it takes,' senior cadet Luter had said...

SHOUT LOUDER

Why do people start talking louder or even start shouting when they are trying to make an impression? A great example of leadership and perception is the first entrance by the chairman of the introduction committee. Everybody is silent and standing at attention. Even the Naval Cadet Corps. One might expect an enormous tirade and it's completely silent at that moment. The contrary turns out to be true. The chairman, very calmly, but firmly and resolutely, makes it clear what he demands from the group. The intonation, the probing gaze, the pauses in his voice, his choice of words, everything hits home. He makes an impression.

This behavior can also be applied on a different level. How does someone embody the role of leader? By screaming loudly and, in this way, trying to enforce authority? Or by sending his message in a calm, yet very resolute way? Indeed, the second way is what works. The leader emanates more power and more authority if he manages to strike the right chord, the right intonation, and the right pauses.

A leadership role is something you have to grow into. Everybody has been in a situation where they were placed in front of a group and expected to take the lead. You feel ill-at-ease and it's obvious to those around you. Still, in such a brief moment and in such a situation, it's all about the appearances you manage to convey! Find the right tone of voice in your communication and display self-confidence. You are no better leader because you start talking louder or because, by coincidence, you stand in front of the group. You are the leader because you know how to communicate, you dare to take decisions and you know how to get the team to work. Your leadership is acknowledged.

In every manner of communication, in every discussion or message that you wish to convey, there are a couple of rules of thumb. As a leader, you need to be aware of these rules. First, there is the so-called *quantity* of the message. How much information is necessary to achieve your objective? Then there is the *quality* of what you say. Is my story correct? After this follows the *relation* to the situation. Is what I have to say relevant? Finally, there is the *style* of what you say. You need to be clear and efficient.[5] If you think these rules of thumb through in advance and you add self-confidence to it, you can hardly go wrong!

> **Building blocks of leadership:**
> *Communicative skills, articulate,*
> *self-confidence*

---

[5] S. Gerritsen - *Een goed gesprek; over communicatieve vaardigheden;* about communicative skills; Nieuwezijds, Amsterdam, 2001

FRESHMEN IN THE AFTERNOON SUN

Somewhere in the distance I could hear a faint humming sound that I could not place. However, it did not belong in my dream. Just as I sub-consciously asked myself what it was that I was hearing, my question was answered by an incredibly loud shriek of '*WAKE UP!*' followed by a very hard beat. What I had heard was the volume of a sound system turned all the way up, waiting for the song to start. Never before had I been jerked out of my sleep so crudely. '*Wake up, boom, boom, boom...*' After having heard the same words and loud beat a couple of times the music stopped and we were ordered to stand in front of the lockers.

There they were again, the same cadets as the night before. This time they were dressed in track gear and they looked remarkably fresh. Obviously, all of us were standing there sleepy in the blue pajamas, looking utterly ridiculous. '*You have exactly one minute to get back in front of the lockers in your sports attire,*' said senior Jacob. '*Execute!*' The group of baroes quickly dispersed to change into their sportswear as soon as possible and exactly one minute later we were headed outside in a long line of cadets, following the Corps' Introduction Committee. This is how they would wake us up every morning from now on.

Following a great session of running across the Den Helder dyke, it was time for breakfast. After three weeks on Texel, no one was put off by a bit of exercise in the morning. Breakfast, on the other hand, that certainly filled us with awe. Three weeks on Texel with no limitations on the quantity of food we wolfed down had ensured that I had develo-ped quite the appetite. However, one of the things in which the Naval Cadets had to educate us was manners, including our table manners. If you did but a single thing wrong in the eyes of a cadet, you would be mercilessly punished. You had to cut your sandwich into six equal parts, without turning your plate. It was not permitted for chocolate sprinkles to fall on your plate. If you were spoken to, you had to lay down your cutlery in the proper way and engage in conversation. If the table was to fall silent, you were considered poor company. In short, you could do nothing right in the eyes of the cadets. Sitting at the head of each table of eight baroes was a cadet of the Introduction Committee.

Unfortunately, there was little time to eat. At the start of a meal, a loud bell would sound, but when you heard this bell again, that sig-naled the end of the meal and you had to lay down your cutlery. This would regularly occur within just a couple of minutes. It was absolutely dreadful if you were about to take your first bite and someone started talking to you because then you had to lay down your cutlery and be a good conversation partner. It was obviously key to try to eat as much as possible, while not being too conspicuous and while still presenting yourself as a proper neighbor at the table. If you did something wrong, you would have to stand on your chair and shout your name followed by the shriek 'I eat like a pig' or something along those lines. Then you would be chewed out by everybody. And just when you thought it was all over and you wanted to take a bite of your food, the bell would sound to end mealtime. The combination of little food, little sleep, physical exertion and a great deal of insecurity caused the moral of the group to drop significantly.

'Everybody in front of the lockers,' we heard throughout the dormitory. I was busy studying the rules of conduct of the Naval Cadet Corps for the umpteenth time. I could recite from memory how to cut a slice of bread, where on my plate I had to position my potatoes, vegetables and meat and how to lay down my cutlery when finished. Rules, rules and more rules. Obviously, some rules would be just slightly different from the regular civilian etiquette which I had learned at home. Placing your cutlery in the proper position when finished is one thing, but you are also obliged to place the knife above the fork, the knife with the cutting edge towards you and the tines of the fork pointing down. You will recognize former naval cadets by this pattern, even to this day.

'Today, baroes, we are going to the rowing and sailing association for naval cadets, the ARZV,' senior cadet Jacob shouted. A wonderfully relaxed Saturday afternoon out on the water, or so I thought. That was just what I needed, but considering the stressful situation we were in as freshmen, somehow I just couldn't believe that we would go on a nice sailing trip across the ponds of the Noord-Holland province. Outside the ARZV, the entire Corps of Naval Cadets, in civilian attire, were waiting for 'us freshies'. There were about twice as many of them as there were of us, so it was about one baroe for every two cadets. Before we knew it, each baroe had a pair of cadets shouting at him.

'WHO ARE YOU,' one of the boys yelled in my ear. *'Hekker,'* I said. *'Hekker who? Baroe Hekker,'* he shouted back. *'Introduce yourself, you lump!!'* So I stood at attention and said *'Baroe Hekker, permission to*

present myself to you, senior sir?' I thought I'd done pretty well there and with a slight sense of pride, I awaited his reaction. It took just a fraction of a second before the next tirade came pouring over me. '*But you are nothing. How would you present yourself then!!??'* he shouted in response. It was quite obvious there were all sorts of one-liners and puns being thrown at us and it was no use trying to avoid them. From the corner of my eye, I could see some of my friends hopping around, beating themselves over the head with a huge inflatable hammer, while shouting '*I am stupid, I am stupid, I am stupid.'* The Corps really went all out with their repertoire of 'funnies' today, the impact of which even caused some of my fellow-baroes to shed some tears here and there.

Just as I entered into a good conversation with a cadet, I got a big blow to the shoulder. '*What are you still doing here, don't you see who's coming over there!'* I saw a big limousine approaching in the distance. 'No idea,' I said in all honesty. '*No idea? No idea?? That is the Senate coming, you lump! Now hurry up and arrange for an honor guard with your class, before the senators disembark!'* I had about twenty seconds to position everybody in an honor guard, have them stand at attention and inform them that this was the senate's vehicle. An impossible task, it seemed but when the Senate got out of the limousine, I acted as if we had been waiting for them, standing at attention and gazing straight ahead. So while everybody dressed in civvies was busy ragging or getting ragged, the senators got out of their vehicle, sharply dressed in their uniforms. Coats and ties, all perfectly in order. The president of the Senate called out to Jacob: 'senior cadet Jacob, please continue what you were doing.' Jacob shouted, '*Carry on,'* across the grounds and the cadets jumped on their baroe like a tiger jumps its prey. The arrival of the Senate and the Chairman of the Introduction Committee had its effect on both us baroes as well as on the Naval Cadet Corps. There was more shouting as each cadet would try to come up with harder and more original ragging methods than the others. Every time someone failed to hold back the tears, that person would be separated from the group. History had shown that it was always possible for excesses to occur, so it had long been established that a supervisory committee should oversee the introduction period. This supervision mostly came from experienced officers who would monitor the activities from the background.

'*So baroe, who are you?'* a cadet asked me. '*Baroe Hekker'* I responded confidently, '*May I make your acquaintance?'* The cadet also stood at attention, shook my hand and said his name. '*Second-year Ruising van Zomer*' he said. 'Ruising van Zomer, Ruising van Zomer,' I repeated quietly in my head, *zomer* being the Dutch word for summer. We started a good-natured conversation. After talking about the Naval College, the ARZV and rugby for a couple of minutes, I wanted to recall his name before finishing the conversation. My mind came to a halt. 'Shit. Second-year, second-year, something with winter in it... Winter, or was it summer? It was one of the seasons. No, winter-something.' Just then, he told me that this had been sufficient and that I could go introduce myself to the rest of the cadets.

It was custom at such a moment to stand at attention and end the conversation with the standard phrase, '*Thank you very much for this introduction second-year or senior,*' followed by his or her name, but there I was. Second-year Ruising van Zomer had indicated that I could end the conversation, 'But how?' I wondered. So instead of ending it awkwardly, I thought of a sneaky way to find out his last name again. '*Before I finish the conversation, I would like permission to ask a question.*' Looking at me doubtfully, second-year Ruising van Zomer nodded his approval, albeit not whole-heartedly. '*Where exactly does your last name come from,*' I asked, with a look of confidence as if to say 'of course I know what your name is.' Second-year Ruising van Zomer seemed caught off guard for a moment, but he quickly parried, '*What exactly do you mean?*' I answered, 'Well, your last name is quite extraordinary and I had never heard it before.' Even before I could finish my sentence, second-year Ruising van Zomer asked, '*So what is my last name then?*' Apparently, he'd had enough time to assess the situation and he countered my smart trick. So there I stood, not knowing what to do. I didn't feel like some stupid ragging activity and decided to gamble.

'*The fact is, second-year,*' I continued, '*yours is such a long last name, I just cannot remember what it is. I do know it has to do with one of the seasons.*' Before I knew it, I was in a push-up position shouting '*I am baroe Hekker and I am not interested in my conversation partner, I am baroe Hekker and I am not interested in my conversation partner.*' Then second-year Ruising van Zomer shouted at me, '*Get up, you lump!*' I quickly jumped up and looked at him. '*You really don't get it, do you?*' he said, somewhat calmer.
I looked as if to say 'What are you talking about?' and he yelled at me '*Who is that behind you!?*'

I turned around and I saw mister Senator, second-year Hamers standing there.

'ATTENTION!' second-year Ruising van Zomer roared.

I jumped at attention and said, *'Baroe Hekker mister senator second-year, permission to make your acquaintance.'*

'WHAT!?' second-year Ruising van Zomer roared in my ear from behind, *'AGAIN!'*

'Second-year mister senator, uhmm, baroe Hekker mister senator, may I, ma...' *'AGAIN!!'*

'Baroe Hekker,' and I realized there was no way out of this for me. I could not remember the senator's name, I didn't know that the second-year was second-year Ruising van Zomer; I didn't know how to introduce myself to a member of the senate.

I accepted the loss and turned toward the screaming cadet, but even before I could apologize for the fact that I could not remember, a cadet who had just come towards us screamed at me that I had turned my back on a member of the Senate. I quickly turned back around and stammered *'Sorry.'*

'SORRY!?' Second-year Ruising van Zomer yelled in my ear again, *'Sorry? Sorry? Sorry is inappropriate, what we say here is 'My apologies'!'*

'ATTENTION!' my latest tormentor yelled at me.

Turning and spinning around as I had, I no longer stood at attention, which is 'obviously' a mortal sin, when you are in front of a member of the Senate. This clearly was one battle lost.

'Second-year Ruising van Zomer and second-year Moorman,' mister senator spoke calmly. *'I can tell the introduction committee has a long way to go yet. This baroe is a very sad case. I presume you will make up for this.'* And off he went.

'Jerk.' I thought. Soon enough, I was walking around in circles on the premises, beating myself over the head with a plastic hammer while yelling *'I am baroe Hekker and I am not interested in the Naval Cadet Corps, I am baroe Hekker and I am not interested in the Naval Cadet Corps.'*

Fortunately, the Senate was getting ready to leave a few minutes later and my name was called to arrange for the escort. I quickly placed a couple of baroes in line in front of the senate's vehicle. Soon after the Senate had left, this ARZV afternoon also came to an end. What could have been a glorious day out in the sun had end in a disaster, a day filled with tears for many, who were asking themselves the important question 'For heaven's sake, what am I doing here?' That night, I was dead-tired when I got into bed. Marc was already in his bunk above me. He whispered, *'What a bloody awful day this was.'* I answered, *'Yes, how'd things go for you?'*

'Oh, I was thrown in the water eight times. Got a lot of comments about my Limburg accent and they thought of me more as a paving stone than a navy officer. Ah well, I guess that's all the more reason to stay.' I couldn't help but smile and think that my afternoon had not been all that bad then, after which I fell into a deep sleep.

WHICH IS THE RIGHT WAY, ACTUALLY?

The CEO of your organization enters the mess hall with a lunch tray. He sits at your table, bows his head over a bowl of soup and without saying a word, he starts slurping his soup. He holds his spoon in his left hand, gripping it in his palm, of course. He rests his left elbow on the table and apparently does not intend to lift it from there. Then he brings his mouth to the spoon. Doesn't the entire image you had of the big CEO fall to pieces at such a time? How do you think this comes across to partners, new clients or international guests? The figurehead of the organization, the leader of the club, unaware of table etiquette? Naturally, there are many forms of etiquette that leaders simply have to master. These are things that will obviously stand out when brought to the dinner table, but which also apply to customary manners. Learning to make introductions during the Corps Introduction Period is not for nothing. You are forced to make acquaintance with people you don't know, but with whom you can be expected to make serious conversation. After all, this is the time for ragging. You have to go through it and you notice it gradually becomes easier. You become more and more confident about engaging in conversation. You are forced to memorize the name of your conversation partner. You are forced to show interest, or in any case, to come across as if you are interested. You are also expected to keep a conversation going. After all, you must be a good 'host'.

In this society, where etiquette and sometimes social standards and values are changing, this society which is becoming increasingly individual, it is in your best interest to assume the highest standard of etiquette from the beginning. Later on, in your interactions, you may always adjust this to a lower standard. This is preferred over not conveying the image you would have wanted to convey as a leader. In addition, you

will feel more confident in unfamiliar surroundings, if you know how things are supposed to be. In any case, this will show your respect for those around you.[6]
It is important for you to be able to create the right image. You are an example to others and they consider you the leader, the diplomat, who, regardless of the circumstances, shall behave as a self-assured role model.

> **Building blocks of leadership:**
> *Etiquette, self-confidence, exemplary*

IT'S OVER

The days flew past. We had classes during the day, as the lectures had begun again, sports in between and a particularly large amount of ragging. The evenings of introducing yourself were the worst of all. The cadets really set out to catch you at any minor mistake. The Senate would regularly walk around there and to stand at attention. You really needed an extra set of eyes in the back of your head.

'Everybody in front of the lockers', was heard once again. After a couple of weeks of Corps Introduction, this had become the routine. *'Follow,'* senior cadet Jacob shouted. The ninety remaining men followed senior cadet Jacob downstairs. At the bottom of the stairs, pillowcases were pulled over our heads and, holding hands, we walked in a long line into the hall. Once inside, we were escorted to our positions. To my left and right, I could hear whispering, which told me there were more cadets present. Then it remained quiet for a while. Utter silence. I could feel my heartbeat in my neck. To my left and right, I could hear feet shifting every now and then. *'BAROES,'* we heard suddenly. I straightened my back again and I could feel the pillowcase over my head was shifting somewhat. *'BAROES,'* again. *'For three weeks you have been learning about the rules of conduct of the Naval Cadet Corps and have made*

---

[6] R. van Dithuyzen - *Hoe hoort het eigenlijk?;* about etiquette and rules of behavior; Becht, Haarlem, 2002

them your own. In three weeks at the Naval College and three weeks on Texel, you have shown to be made of the right stuff. You have spent six weeks away from home, living in insecurity and sometimes going through moments you don't care to recollect but believe me, you have become different people from the civilians who took their first steps inside the Royal Netherlands Naval College. Therefore, ladies and gentlemen of the class of '97, it pleases me to welcome you to the Naval Cadet Corps. The Corps Introduction has now come to an end.' At that moment, the pillowcase was pulled off my head and we were applauded from all sides. I saw my classmates standing around me, flanked by a senior-cadet. *'Hi there, Jochen,'* the senior cadet said to me, *I'm your sea father.'* I had no idea what was going on. I saw happy faces everywhere. Cadets walking around congratulating everyone. The music was resonating through the room and outside the barbecues were being preheated. After six weeks of highs and lows, I had now entered the Naval Cadet Corps.

2. THE COLLEGE

Knowledge is proud that it knows so much,
wisdom is humble that it knows no more.
- William Cowper - (1731 - 1800)

The cadets learn what leadership is from the beginning. In fact, they learn them along with the practical nautical skills, since, as an up and coming naval officer, you actually are in charge of the bridge of a naval vessel. You are continuously assessed based on your leadership skills. This assessment causes even more stress. This chapter is an introduction to the first practical skills of leadership for officer trainees. In addition, the element of stress is looked at in detail. These will be moments when all eyes are on you.

STUDY, PRACTICE SPORT, STUDY

All of the freedom of being a cadet took some getting used to after the Corps Introduction. The freedom to do things like eat whatever and whenever you wanted. There were meals at fixed times in the cadets' restaurant, of course, but you could get candy from the vending machine when you felt like it, or have a coke without worrying about who might barge in on you. On the weekends, it was up to you at what time you got out of bed. There were so many things that I had taken for granted and I now realized how wonderful they actually were. Life at the Naval College consisted of three things: study, the Corps and sports. The Naval College is a Military boarding school, where you were required to study hard. Failing an exam would mean taking it again. If you failed the make-up exam, you would get a yellow card. Two yellow cards would get you kicked out and you could say goodbye to your naval career. The school had five different degree programs: the Administrative Corps, the Naval Corps, the Technical Service Corps, the Electrical Engineering Services Corps and the Marine Corps. The study load at the Marine Corps and the Administrative Corps was low, compared to the many study hours required for the Technical Service Corps and the Electrical Engineering Services Corps. The Naval Corps covered a little bit of both, through a combination of the more difficult math subjects, like the 'alpha' subjects, and social subjects. I had chosen to take the Naval Corps degree program. Besides general management skills, mathematics, physics, English and Dutch we were educated in nautical skills such as geometry, navigation and astronomy. The study load was high from the start. Having been redubbed junior cadets, we had to find our own rhythm and properly divide the days of the week. Some matters were fixed. You could not get around the timetable of the classes, but also, every morning at eight o'clock sharp, rain or shine, there would be an inspection of each platoon, to check whether the uniforms were proper, whether the shoes were shined and whether you had shaved according to the required standard.

This military ceremony often lasted until ten past eight, after which everyone was expected to be in class at exactly quarter past eight.

Classes continued after lunch and often around five, you were free to go. You were then finally allowed to shed coat and tie. The boarding school offered a minimum of privacy. The juniors at the Naval College would share one large dormitory all through their first year. In order to study, you could use a small room in one of the outbuildings. Promotion to the second year meant you would share a bedroom and a study room. These small rooms were in a separate building for second-year and senior-year cadets. As a senior, you had your own bedroom in which to both sleep and study. Privacy, therefore, depended on the number of years you had passed at the Royal Netherlands Naval College.

After class, there was plenty of opportunity to go practice sports. The Naval College had excellent sporting facilities: three tennis courts, a football pitch, a sports gymnasium with a squash court, fitness room, boxing and fencing arena and a sauna. You could also use the local sports facilities, like the rugby field at the local rugby club or the Den Helder swimming pool. The dilemmas would mostly present themselves in the evening: which sporting activity to choose from and where to eat. And so the days at the Naval College flew by on a fixed schedule.

INNER DISCIPLINE
We had roll call every morning at eight o'clock, regardless of rain, snow or hail, no matter if you had slept poorly or if it just wasn't your day. Every morning means every morning. Moreover, you couldn't just pop

out of bed at five minutes to eight, jump into some ragbag outfit and a pair of worn out shoes for roll call. No, this was about making sure you looked your absolute best. The uniform was to be neat, the shirt ironed, and the tie straight. You were to be clean and freshly showered, properly shaven and with a shoe shine in which you could almost see your face. And ready at eight o'clock. Why? Because that is how it's supposed to be. Your classmates, your fellow corps members, they are all there too, after all. It is the general rule of conduct.

It is quite something, having to point out to your classmates that their shoes haven't been properly shined, or they should do a better job shaving. It is a challenge not to make yourself too unpopular with the group. The only way to achieve this is to be consistent and set a good example yourself. If your mate has not shined his shoes well enough and the person next to him hasn't either, you must point this out to both of them. You will lose all authority, if you fail to shine your own shoes properly and then go pointing out to others that they have failed in this. Leadership means setting a good example. As a leader, people will always be looking to you. They look at what you do, at how you do it and they listen to what you say.[7]

Besides this, you will want to emanate something, when wearing a uniform or a tailor-made suit. It is your inner discipline that ensures you look your sharpest in a suit. How awkward does it look when people wear a suit and then match it with shoes that haven't been shined, or with a wrinkled shirt? That is just inappropriate. It doesn't fit! Sure, you can remain unshaven and just put on sweatpants on any given Sunday and read a paper at the table, but your inner discipline will ensure that everything is neatly in order come Monday morning. You behave the way you look and this is what you emanate.

> **Building blocks of leadership:**
> *Obliging, consistent, exemplary*

---

[7] J. Aidar – Develop your leadership skills; Kogan Page, London 2011

ANNUAL PARTY

'*Junior cadet Jansen has no saddle on his bike.*' The words reverberated through the main building. The broadcasts of the internal cadet radio station during the 'dayshift' were indeed quite a bit more civilized in nature, than those of the 'nightshift'. Every hour of the day, a different duo of cadets would play records for us, twenty-four duos per day, which could only be heard in the main building of the Naval College. While half the Naval Cadet Corps was at work getting the décor for the annual ball ready in time, the other half was sleeping in the dormitory. Every year, the Naval Cadet Corps organized a four-day gala called 'the Assaut', which is a French word that refers to a fencing match. Every year, a different theme was used. The corps chose an 'Assaut Committee' early in the year and the committee distributed the various projects among the senior-year cadets, who were placed in charge of a certain area of the main building. In two weeks' time, the entire main building of the Naval College was transformed into the specific theme of the Assaut. All cadets were assigned to various projects, either in a dayshift or a nightshift. Under the direction of a senior cadet, the different areas were turned into magical rooms, ballrooms or even a theatre. Every detail was thoroughly addressed. Extra floors were added, as were fountains, bars or seating areas. All sorts of arrangements were made for a proper party or an impressive décor. It was a particular challenge for the project managers to steer everything in the right direction while distributing the 'handy' cadets over several different projects. The cadets had to apply their organizational skills and leadership.

During the day, the work could be done in a fairly structured manner, because the Naval College board was present. At night, there was no holding back. Every evening, a different cadet would be nailed to the dance platform, in his blue fatigues, dozens of nails pierced through it, sticking him to the stage. The second-year and senior cadets obviously already knew all about these shenanigans and the juniors were fast learners. The internal radio broadcast was taken full advantage of for bidding on having people nailed down. Most of the time, the cadets would use beer for their bidding wars. There were requests for songs to be played as well, poems were read about fellow corps members and other, often embarrassing tales were told. In these two weeks, it became all too clear where you stood in the Corps. It didn't matter how big or strong you were, once you were targeted by others, they would nail you to the stage in your blue fatigues and you would be a regular subject of a 'poem'.

After two weeks of hard work, bar nights with DJs in some dark base-
ment and hoping to not get nailed down, it was time for the Assaut, four
days of festivities. Thursday was the shortest day to party. It was an
evening to express gratitude to the regular staff at the Naval College. One
night's worth of partying was supposed to wipe the slate clean of all the
miserable times in the mess halls, dormitories and the main building. I
wonder if this was ever successful. Friday was the more official day of
the gala. This is when the high-ranking naval officers were invited, as
well as several Dutch student bodies, the Senate of the Royal Military
Academy and even the royal family.

The dress was white tie, including all sorts of accessories and full length
skirts for the ladies. Friday night was always a very formal occasion.
The cadets were expected to mingle with the invited guests and display
what excellent hosts they were. Most of the time, the high-profile guests
would leave in time for the gala to turn into a 'cadet party'. Friday was
also the first evening when the cadets were expected to bring along a
'fairy'. The fairies are the dates of the male cadets, often young ladies
who had been suddenly thrown into the deep end of the Naval College.
Considering the high-ranking guests and the specific invitations, the
fairies were required to dress in accordance with the prescribed etiquette,
which meant at least ankle-length dresses. The gentlemen cadets were
urged to make sure their fairies complied and as a standard, there would
be dresses available at the door for any ladies who as yet failed to follow the dress code. There would be people stationed at the entrance to
specifically check up on this and no matter how embarrassing, ladies
who arrived in skirts that did not meet the length of this dress code were
kindly requested to change into a skirt from the Naval College. Imagine
you are an 18-year old, attending a gala for the first time, for which your
new boyfriend has given specific instructions and your mother insists
that your old dress is just fine for the occasion. You trust your mother's
opinion to take one dress with you for Friday and Saturday and then you
arrive at the door and are asked to change your dress. How embarrassing
this must be. Many enthusiastic starts to what should be a wonderful
weekend will have been dampened by this. The embarrassed look from
her, the looks of reproach from him.

The Saturday of the Assaut was all about the naval cadets. This was the
Corps' party. No fancy guests, just the regular officers and the cadets with
their fairies. The dress code was black tie for the men and knee-length

skirts for the ladies. No matter how much fun Friday evening was, the real party was always on Saturday. After two weeks of hard work, a couple of days of festivities and two days of taking down everything and cleaning up again, the Naval Cadet Corps had managed to show the outside world their good side. However, the party itself obviously contained many learning objectives. The cadets had continued to gain experience.

> **Building blocks of leadership:**
> *Organizational capacity, etiquette,*
> *social conscience*

STRESS ON THE BRIDGE SIMULATOR

After the Assaut, the days flew by, with classes, sports and corps activities. Where the emphasis was on the academic side of the program in the first year, in the second year the attention shifted more to the practical side and leadership. Several cadets were chosen for committee functions within an association. Naturally, the senior cadets would hold the most appealing positions like chairperson, treasurer or secretary, while the second-years would hold the position of 'member'. An additional obstacle was included in the training program: the bridge simulator. As future naval officers, we were expected to demonstrate our navigation skills on both the bridge simulator and on the training vessel called 'Zeefakkel' (Dutch for Sea Torch).

Cadets sweating it out on the bridge simulator.

There were microphones and cameras fitted all over the bridge simulator. As an officer of the watch on the bridge, you were expected to lead your team and be able to steer a safe course. In short, you had to be able to prioritize. During these bridge simulator sessions, which would last an entire morning or afternoon, you were constantly being evaluated. This was quite stressful for many cadets. You were expected to be able to put all the theoretical knowledge you had acquired into practice, including navigation regulations, navigation itself, radar operation, and the metrics of the earth. On this day, I had the task of acting as officer of the watch and taking the lead on the navigation bridge. It was a sunny morning when I entered the bridge simulator, a couple of nautical charts stuck under my arm.

The simulator was built like the bridge of a naval vessel. The view you had of the outside, however, was a computer animation, but you could hear the wind blowing and feel the bridge moving as with the surging water of the sea. This was obviously controlled by large hydraulic pumps, installed underneath the 'bridge', which would make the simulator move up and down. Right now, the fluorescent tubes were still on and from the lack of moving vessels around us, I gathered that we were in the traffic separator of Texel. A traffic separator was nothing but a scheme of fictional highways with fixed shipping routed. You were obliged to remain sailing inside certain 'lanes'. '*Good morning gentlemen*' said the navigation officer in charge of assessing this session. '*I believe today you will sail within the traffic separation system of Texel and Hekker will be in charge, am I right?*' '*Certainly, sir,*' I replied with confidence. '*Great, then I suggest you start on your briefing in twenty minutes and until then, you can prepare the bridge,*' the officer continued. He then left the bridge and went into the control room. The control room was, in fact, the nerve center of the bridge simulator. From here, everything was controlled, simulated and monitored. It had a large window with a full view of the entire bridge simulator. I had twenty minutes. I asked one of my team members to prepare the radar and another one to go through the checklists and keep me posted on any special circumstances. I walked over to the chart table and unfolded my nautical chart. The route I had to draw on the chart was not that difficult, but various ships would probably challenge me, as well as fishing boats sailing around my destination. I went through the route again in my mind, thinking about a shallow section here, about what my arrival time would be and about what speed I should set. The door to the bridge simulator opened

51

and there was the officer with a checklist under his arm. *'Ready?'* he asked. *'Certainly, sir.'* I called my five classmates for a briefing. *'Good morning,'* I said. *'Today, we will sail through a traffic separation scheme (TSS).'* I pointed out the route to be taken with my calipers. *'Bas, you'll be behind the radar and I expect you to report when a ship's course will take it to within less than 1,500 yards from us.'* I continued my briefing with instructions to Sjoerd, Mark and Alrik and concluded by saying, *'Alex, you'll be at the helm. Are there any questions?'* They all shook their heads. Apparently, I had been clear. *'Do you have any questions commander?'* I asked the assessor. *'No, I don't, officer cadet Hekker,'* he said, *'Let us begin.'* As he walked to the control room, the fluorescent lights went out, the sound was switched on and the bridge started to move. *'Commence run,'* was heard over the intercom. *'Helmsman, set eighty rotations, both axles.'* I said firmly. *'Eighty rotations both,'* Alex repeated, pushing the propeller buttons. From the corner of my eye, I checked the displays and they indeed indicated eighty rotations on both axles. *'Port twenty,'* I said, meanwhile checking the panels to confirm the rudders were indeed turning left at a twenty degree angle, *'Port twenty,'* Alex repeated. *'Port rudder at twenty,'* he said, just a fraction later. *'Steer course zero-seven-three,'* and the frigate turned left, into the TSS.

I quickly walked one round of the bridge, together with my two lookouts, in order to identify all other visible ships. Just as I was thinking how smoothly this was going, the phone rang. *'Bridge,'* I said. *'Yes good morning sir, this is the Engine Room, we would like to carry out maintenance on the starboard main engine. I trust it's no problem if we place that on standby for a while?'* The assessor said this so amicably that I was almost inclined to say yes, immediately. Fortunately, I checked myself just in time and asked, *'How will this affect me?'* *'Well sir, you'll only have one axle at your disposal, so your speed will be limited to sixty-five rotations on the remaining axle.'* I quickly checked my 'smart list' and saw that with these speed settings, I would reach the rendezvous point just in time but we would not be able to afford any mishaps whatsoever. *'Why is it necessary to do this now?'* I asked. *'Well sir, it's maintenance, you know? The basis of our propulsion.'* My mind raced for a split-second, *'We are currently on course through the TSS and we have to make it to our rendezvous. Let's postpone this maintenance for an hour.'* *'Aye-aye sir, as you wish,'* he said and hung up the phone. *'Officer of the watch, lookout here,'* said Alrik. *'Lookout, come in,'* I said, indicating he had my attention. *'I have a contact on green fifty,'* Alrik said as he gave the coordinates. I grabbed my visors and considered what he had said. 'Contact on green fifty' means on our starboard side. Hmmm, according to this information, this could turn out to be a collision course.' *'Radar, what's your view of this contact?'* *'I have no contact on radar there, officer of the watch,'* Bas said, his head nearly buried inside the radar cabinet. *'You don't see anything?'* I asked, *'Negative, sir. I have the right settings. I turned all switches and adjusted the settings, but I see no contact there,'* Bas responded, a bit hesitant. I checked his settings and, indeed, they looked perfect. *'Lookout Mark,'* I said, *'could you call the engine control room and ask them to send someone to check the radar performance?' 'Certainly sir,'* Mark said, and he quickly picked up the phone. I felt that my priority should be with the fishing boat at that moment and that I should go out and take a good look myself to see what was really going on, rather than fuss over the radar settings. *'Officer of the watch, the radar is working again and I have a good view of the contact on screen now. The distance is four miles and he will pass our stern at 300 yards.'* The radar automatically measured the distance to be observed to other ships with the current course and speed. I needed to think quickly. 300 yards astern. If I added some speed, the ship would pass our stern at an even further distance. I gave Alex the instructions to pick up some speed and he repeated what I'd said, carrying out the order. *'The fishing boat now passes our stern at 1,200 yards, officer of the watch,'* Bas told me. I thought for a moment, picked up the phone and dialed four sixes. *'Commander,'* I heard at the other end. *'Commander, this is the officer of the watch. I have a fishing boat on green fifty at a distance of four miles. He is busy with his catch and will pass astern at 1,200 yards in eight minutes. I'm okay with that and intend to proceed with the current course and speed.' 'Okay, thank you,'* the commander said, *'Proceed.'* I continued my course and speed, certain I would make it to the rendezvous on time.

Suddenly, all of the lights went on, the movement of the bridge stopped and the sound ceased. *'End of exercise,'* came through the speakers. I looked at my watch and saw that it was almost lunchtime. Time had really flown by. *'Okay boys, everybody gather round please,'* said the officer who had come out of the control room. *'How do you think it went?'* Everyone nodded in satisfaction and I nodded along with them. What a relief for this to be over. I was sweating like a pig, despite having only sailed a short distance. I wondered what it would be like when I would have to handle an actual crisis on a real ship. *'I think it went well,'* the officer said. *'Fine preparations, good, clear and understandable advance briefing. The right priorities set while sailing. In short, a very clean run! Enjoy your meal.'* I let out a huge sigh of relief, packed my stuff and thought to myself that it had gone pretty well indeed.

DEALING WITH STRESS

The sessions on the bridge simulator were quite stressful for the cadets. Unfortunately, it is quite difficult to give advice on the best way to deal with stress. This is different for every individual. In Chapter Six, I provide a tool that you may use as a guide. In any case, as a leader, it is important for you to be able to manage stress. In times of stress, everyone will be looking to you. This is when the leader rises.

You obviously cannot predict how you may react under certain circumstances, but everyone has been faced with stressful situations in their life and sometimes responded adequately, sometimes not. Your ability to deal with stress depends on the situation. These are learning opportunities. Perhaps you have been sleeping poorly for the past couple of nights, or you haven't been feeling well lately. Even so, you are still the leader! You have to be there when it counts. When the increase of adrenaline reduces the ability of others to make the right decisions, you are exactly the one who must execute the decisions in a clear, consistent and particularly effective manner. Stress is also defined as a lack of mental room to maneuver.[8] It stops you from seeing solutions, which is evidenced both physically and mentally. One recent trend aimed at dealing with stress is 'Mindfulness'. Mindfulness asks that you pause in order be present in reality, directing conscious attention to the task at hand, allowing you to handle it with more freedom.[9] In a more concrete sense, Mindfulness will ensure that you stop, look and act. It is but one example among many designed to help you deal with stress. Whichever method you chose, make sure that you are aware of yourself and your boundaries, allowing yourself to adjust these boundaries when necessary.

---

[8] Prof. Dr. L.U. de Sitter - *Synergetisch produceren; Human Resources Mobilisation in de productie; een inleiding in de structuurbouw;*
Synergetic production, about HR Mobilisation in production, a managerial substantiation and methodology for integral redesign of production systems; Van Gorcum, Assen, 2000

[9] E. Maex - *Werken met Mindfulness; basisoefeningen*; about working with Mindfulness using basic exercises; Lannoo, Tielt, 2008

SERVING AS A LEADER

On the bridge simulator, the officer of the watch has a responsibility to set an example and to act as leader. For naval officers, practical skills are a particular test of leadership. Leadership skills are tested against a yardstick that is constantly being raised.

Setting an example means demonstrating that there is always work to be done. When practicing skills using the bridge simulator, you are constantly aware that next time, someone else will be giving the orders. This means that everyone involved is obliged to put in their best effort. You will set the bar high, of course! You will clearly point out to the people on your team what you expect. Managing expectations this way, is important for all leaders. This is why the objective must be clear. The entire staff must be aware of the goal; it creates a sense of commitment to the process. In the simple scenarios presented on the bridge simulator, the objective was to reach a certain location at a previously determined time. By creating a sense of commitment among the crew, they will feel obliged to think with you. As a leader, it should be your goal to make the best use of the particular skills of your crew. When people feel that they are helping you to address obstacles in the way of a known objective, they will feel greater commitment to the desk and will produce better results. The key to leadership is to involve your people in the process and eventually to dare to make decisions on your own. You are responsible for the ambitious goal that you have set. It should be clear that you have high expectations regarding the outcome as well as the contribution and commitment of your team.

One type of leadership is 'servant leadership'. It stipulates that a leader must be willing to 'serve' in order to be a good leader. The concepts 'serving' and 'leading' are therefore considered equivalent. *Servant leadership* is not a leadership style, but rather a life philosophy - how

55

one must 'be'.[10] One particularly positive aspect of servant leadership is that it presumes that your personal growth will also help others to grow. In this way, you will grow along with the organization. This style of leadership is not all positive, however. Sometimes a leader cannot merely serve, or put other people's interests above one's own. There are times when a leader needs to take a firm stand, making decisions that are not popular, but that are in the best interests of the organization. The servant leader is socially conscious, placing the 'other' at the center. In my opinion, a leader should strive for this, but he will not always be able to live up to it.

> **Building blocks of leadership:**
> *People-oriented, team builder,*
> *demanding, ambitious*

PROCESSING INFORMATION AND SETTING PRIORITIES

The advantage of the '*Zeefakkel*', the training vessel of the Royal Netherlands Naval College, compared to the bridge simulator, was that the *Zeefakkel* was a real ship at sea. No one was able to influence the sea traffic around you. Most often, this was a more relaxed environment to work in than the bridge simulator. The only problem I had were the awful odors. One day of sailing the *Zeefakkel* would provide you with so many bad smells and heavy seas, that nine out of ten cadets would be scrambling over the guardrail to donate their breakfast or lunch to the fish. Because of the wind around the ship, much of the stomach content would end up blowing back against the ship's hull or onto the deck. Combine this with the smell of fish and seawater, the diesel fumes from the engine room, the food being prepared in the galley and the hand-rolled cigarettes that the commander smoked and you were certain to have your own stomach churning as well. In fact, it took a lot of the fun out of sailing. However, if in between the moments of seasickness you managed to set the right priorities while sailing, the atmosphere onboard would be calmer and allow you more time to make good decisions. Still, it is interesting to see how differently people prioritize and deal with pressure.

---

[10] Dr. I. Nuijten - Servant-Leadership; Paradox or Diamond in the Rough?
A Multidimensional Measure and Empirical Evidence – doctoral thesis 2011

Everyone has a certain maximum capacity for the processing of information. In general, there is not a whole lot of difference between individuals. Most adults are capable of storing seven different elements in their memory at one time. George Miller introduced this theory as early as 1956. People with an especially high capacity will perhaps manage nine and those with a poor capacity will be able to store roughly five elements.[11]

Why then does it seem as though some people experience information overload after having only one order issued to them, while others never seem to have this problem? The answer is simple. People who never seem to be overwhelmed by information are better able to prioritize effectively. They have the ability to push less important information to the background while focusing on what really needs attention now. The analytical capacity of the individual dictates how well they will be able to prioritize.

Advanced knowledge and experience will obviously help an individual to assess situations more quickly, but a helpful trick is to ask yourself 'What must I do now?' This question will make it easier for you to set the right priorities and to analyze the situation properly.

'*WHAT* must I do now?' Focusing on the '*what*' forces you think about the real task that needs to be performed. Ensure that the task is clear. If it is not clear, you will need to retrieve information actively in order to clarify the '*what*'.

'What *MUST* I do now?' Ask yourself what you *must* really do. Are there matters that do not immediately need to be addressed, but which you would like to address?

'What must *I* do now?' Must you indeed do it yourself or are there perhaps others who could take over your task? You will often notice that the number of tasks you really need to do yourself is very limited. When in a leadership position, there are many tasks that could be delegated to others.

---

[11] Prof. Dr. J.B. Asendorpf – *Psychologie van de persoonlijkheid*; about personality psychology; Springer media, Heidelberg, 2009

'What must I do *NOW*?' Is there indeed a time limit for the task you are facing, or could it be postponed to a later time? What will happen if the task is finished later? Who has set the deadline and for what reason? In the end, you will have to do, perform, take action.

If you go through your list of tasks with these questions in mind, it will be easier for you to prioritize the actions that really must be carried out now. However, just understand where the priorities lie, calms things down considerably. Calm will create internal room to maneuver, which will greatly reduce the chance of stress. After all, nobody wants a leader to be stressed.

Officers in training are taught to deal with stress and to set priorities from the very beginning. The officer of the watch, for example, is overloaded with messages. He must simultaneously deal with a phone call from the commander, new information from his crew, a request from the engine room to perform maintenance on the propulsion, surrounding traffic trying to sail right through you and more. These scenarios all start out small and relatively easy, but they will soon grow and become more complex. Increased knowledge and experience will help you to create more internal room to maneuver. The more that is demanded of you, the more information you will be able to process. Based on knowledge and experience, you will know what information is important and what may be pushed to the bottom of your list of priorities. 'What must I do now?' can be a handy tool to analyze the situation.

> **Building blocks of leadership:**
> *Analytical capacity, prioritizing, ability to delegate, knowledge, experience*

3. FALL DOWN, GET UP, AND CARRY ON

How much more grievous are the consequences of anger than the causes of it.
- Marcus Aurelius - (121 - 180)

No one ever wins in a conflict situation, especially not in a conflict situation that escalates; when two parties have been unable to adapt themselves, to conform to the other, or to bend the situation to suit their needs. In a hierarchy, it is easy to claim that the subordinate is at fault, but, is this always the case? Is it not the responsibility of the superior to get his people to perform at their best? Still, there are often positives to draw from negative experiences. You learn about yourself, but you also learn how *not* to lead. Unpleasant as they may be, these lessons will also increase your internal room to maneuver, helping you to become a better leader.

GETTING ACQUAINTED

I took a walk through the ship after having filled out a lot of paperwork in a small office. I was somewhere below deck on a beautiful multipurpose frigate. She was about 400 feet in length, with a crew of approximately 140. The ship was fitted with all sorts of conveniences - a baker, cooks, multiple places for the crew to relax and of course a gym and sleeping quarters. In short, this was a floating village. However, floating village that it may have been, its primary use was for crisis situations. For this reason, the luxury is limited to a minimum and the frigate is equipped with a score of weapons systems to carry out its tasks. Fortunately, I had sailed on this type of frigate before, and I knew my way around the ship as I had been on one for four months. Only the name of the ship and the people on board were different this time.

The multipurpose frigate of the Royal Netherlands Navy.

My first visit was to my manager, the head of Operations, Lieutenant Commander Maarten.[12] I went up a couple of stairs and knocked on the side of the open door to his cabin. *'Come in.'* I pushed a curtain aside and crossed the high threshold. The 10'x10' cabin had a desk, a bunk bed and a washbasin. In the corner, a door led to a shower room, which was shared with the adjacent cabin. The other walls were covered with large closets. Unused space was really an unnecessary luxury on board a navy vessel. *'Good afternoon sir, I am Lieutenant Hekker.'* *'Ah, Jochen,'* Maarten said, as he pushed a chair towards me and stuck out his hand. I shook his hand and sat down in the desk chair.

During our conversation, Maarten told me that I would be replacing the 'oldest officer of the watch', the most experienced officer in the group of young officers with the responsibilities of navigating and keeping watch on the bridge. They are assigned the task of safely sailing the ship in rotating shifts of four hours. I hoped expectations would not be too high in the beginning and I indicated that I might need to get 'warmed up' somewhat, to get back up to standard. It was a pleasant talk, in which we pointed out our mutual expectations and after half an hour, Maarten took me to meet the commanding officer.

We went up a flight of stairs again and reached the cabin. *'This is the commander's quarters. Just wait here, I'll see if he has time,'* Maarten said. He knocked on the wall of the cabin and waited until he heard *'Come in'*, before pushing the curtain aside. *'Commander,'* Maarten said, *'I would like to introduce you to Lieutenant Hekker, our new officer of the watch.'* *'Ah yes, send him in,'* I heard the commander say. For the first time, I stepped into the commander's cabin. 'Jochen Hekker,' I said and shook his hand. In front of me stood a man in his late forties, about 5'9".

My first impression of him was not what I had expected it to be. I had expected an eloquent, assertive, enthusiastic, and attentive naval officer to be in command of this magnificent ship. Maybe I had expected to be greeted more warmly. However, none of this was the case. *'Take a seat, Jochen,'* he pointed at the large dining table in the cabin. His steward had walked in and he filled the commander's mug with coffee. I was given a saucer and cup, which the steward filled as well. The

---

[12] See appendix 2 for the ranks and positions of the Royal Navy

commander got up from behind his desk and joined me at the table. On his mug, I saw a large Ajax emblem, one of the best soccer clubs in the Netherlands. *'Well, I hope you have more knowledge of sailing than you do of soccer,'* I said with a big smile. I was a soccer fan, but not a fan of Ajax. I figured a joke like this might be a good icebreaker. The commander gave me a grumpy look, thought about how to react to this, and then looked at his open notebook and ignored my remark. Ouch, that was awkward. The rest of our conversations that afternoon were equally as bad. I did my utmost to present myself as best I could, I emphasized that I wanted to succeed, wanted to work hard and hoped to learn a lot, but it was all in vain. Not a word of encouragement, no reassurance, not a smile, nothing! I had regretted the Ajax-remark the moment I spoke the words. I usually also like make fun of that club by referring to them in combination with the brand of soap by the same name, but this time I was happy that I had kept that to myself.

Later on, in my cabin, I thought about the two introductory talks and it seemed to me that Maarten was a nice guy, but not the one to rely on when you go to war. The commander seemed anything but nice. We just didn't click, but I had every intention of changing this. I was determined to make my stay onboard a good one and to learn all of the tricks of the trade.

THE DECK IS SHUFFLED

'Officer of the watch,' the commander called across the bridge. *'What are these ships coming out of the port?'* 'Ships coming out of port?' I thought to myself, the port is nine miles north by north-west. I was confused. We were doing an exercise off the south coast of England and I was busy navigating safely, evading ships around us and trying to stay on top of the aerial threat. *'No idea, commander,'* I said and turned around, directing the lookout. *'Officer of the watch, GET OVER HERE!'* he roared across the bridge. All the conversations on the bridge fell silent and I walked back to the commander. All eyes and ears were focused on the conversation that was about to take place. Altogether, there were about twenty-five men on the bridge. During exercises like this one, or when sailing got a little more tense, the bridge would fill up with personnel. Two people for external communication, a helmsman, two lookouts, Chief of Operations Maarten, the Navigator, the commander and all sorts of other people who were required to be on the bridge for various reasons. *'What are these ships, officer of the watch?'* the commander shouted, this time while I was really close to him. *'I don't know yet, sir,'* I said, emphasizing the word 'yet', since I had given that same response not a minute ago. This time I had the presence of mind to say *'I will find out for you, Commander.'* *'What do you mean, find out? Find out what? You are the officer of the watch. You're supposed to know this!'* I thought hard and I was certain that these ships were not part of the current exercise. The ships involved in the exercise were all around us and I knew perfectly well what their positions were. *'Nice preparations, then.'* His words resonated sarcastically across the bridge. I crawled over to the chart table to mark the position on the chart. Maarten stood behind me, looking over my shoulder. *'What are those ships Maarten?'* I asked him. *'No idea,'* he whispered. *'They have nothing to do with this exercise.'* 'Indeed not, friend,' I thought to myself. 'You might've said so just now. After all, you are the head of the department and you should have stood up for me.' We discovered later that there was another military squadron leaving the port of Plymouth about twelve miles from our exercise. I could have gotten this information from something called *a port order* from Plymouth, had I prepared better, according to the commander. None of my experienced colleagues knew what these ships were doing and nobody had ever checked port orders from nearby ports prior to an exercise before. However, it was clear to me that the commander had high standards and I was not spared because of my lack of experience. I was new on board, but the rest of the crew

already had a number of weeks under their belts. In fact, the biggest clue about what was to come should have been Maarten's reaction. He allowed his own personnel to be chewed out over a question that he did not know the answer to himself.

PATHETIC ENGINEER

'Officer of the watch,' the commander called from his seat next to the helmsman, a couple of days later. *'Yes commander,'* I responded. *'What is the tangent value of 30?'* *'The tangent value of 30,'* I repeated. *'You must mean the sine or cosine value, sir?'* That I knew off the top of my head, since you need these calculations to maneuver the ship. *'No, the tangent value of 30,'* he said once again. *'Helmsman, starboard twenty,'* I shouted at that instant. We were in the middle of a maneuvering exercise and I was again acting as officer of the watch. In order to monitor yourself during the maneuver, you're constantly taking bearings of the reference ship. In combination with the distance, you will be able to see whether you are on track to get into the right position. This is stressful and when the bridge is packed, you need to concentrate on doing things right. This is when the commander decided to ask me this question. For a split-second, I lost my concentration, but I quickly pulled myself together and gave my orders to the helmsman. I dove behind the compass and saw that I was off my ideal course line.

'Officer of the watch, can I get an answer?' the commander shouted again. *'Not now commander, I am busy. I'll get back to you on that.'* He then started laughing loudly and he shouted across the bridge: *'Some pathetic engineer you are.'* He got out of his chair and, with a look of contempt, walked off the bridge in the middle of this important maneuvering exercise. You could hear a pin drop on the bridge and I was certain I looked like a fool. Fortunately, the busy exercise prevented me from lingering on the matter. Apart from this one small move, the exercise went fairly well. A couple of minutes later, the exercise ended and all of the vessels were again able to set their own course and speed. I moved out of formation with the other ships and thanked everyone for their efforts.

'Clean exercise Jochen,' said Maarten, who came to stand next to me. I stood in the middle of the bridge behind the helmsman, thinking about the remarks from the commander. *'Very good exercise,'* Maarten repeated. I looked at him, *'What is the tangent value of 30?'* *'Yeah, well, I really*

didn't understand it either.' He turned around and walked off the bridge. Obviously, the tone for the coming months had been set.

CORRECTING, COMPLIMENTING, AND TAKING PUNCHES

It is remarkably easy to attack people. But what do you hope to achieve with this? Maybe you'll make a few people laugh, but you will lose face, especially as a leader. The leader is supposed to be the one who knows how to act as a coach and who is able to boost the self-confidence of his employees. Indeed, if things go well, or if an employee gives an outstanding performance, everybody should hear about it. If you feel, however, that an employee needs to be corrected, admonished or given additional direction, you should approach the person separately and address the issue one-on-one. Employees will then be more inclined to accept your feedback and criticism. After all, he doesn't need to be shamed in front of all the others who are witness to his failure. In this way, he can fully concentrate on your criticism and use it to improve his performance. Those who laugh along with you don't do it because you're funny. They all realize that this sneering laughter may someday be directed at them. A leader does not need his people to find him funny.

A leader should be demanding, but he can never lose his sense of reality. If your people are not performing to your standards, there are multiple ways to get them to where you want them to be. Should you have someone leading you, you will also need to be resilient. You will need to know yourself very well and be aware of your limits. You should never allow yourself to be put down when things are not going your way, not even when the boss is too strong in giving direction.

A crew should see a leader as 'the leader', as the one who steps out in front of the situation, the one who coaches and directs them when necessary, and especially as the one who makes the team and the individuals better. This is the type of leader who people will acknowledge and who they will want to follow. That leader has justified his leadership.

> **Building blocks of leadership:**
> *Self-knowledge, demanding, resilience*

MOTHER GOOSE

On all visits to foreign ports, we followed the same ritual. The rental car of the commander arrived and the commander would step outside and walk down the gangway, followed at an appropriate distance by all of the department heads - the head of Technical Service, the head of Logistics, the head of Operations and the First Officer. Traditionally, when the commander disembarks or embarks, an announcement is made over the ship's PA system. The announcement is a signal for everyone who is 'in sight' to drop whatever they are doing and stand at attention for the commander. This is why the department heads would walk a certain distance behind the commander. It made him look like a mama duck with all of her ducklings following in her wake. The commander would always get in the driver's seat and the rest of the department heads would decide on the spot who would sit where. It probably had to do with the mounting tension between the commander and myself, but I found the submissive behavior of the department heads extremely annoying. Nobody dared to stand up to him at all. My annoyance was exacerbated by the fact that the new 'senior officer of the watch' seemed to be a kiss ass, in my opinion. 'Yes commander, no commander, of course commander.' He once told me that it is better to walk around the ship with books under your arm, because then it looked like you were doing something. I could not believe my ears and I told him he was crazy. Why would you go around with books under your arm, if you don't need them? I am sure he was thinking that I could say whatever I wanted, but that he was not the one on the commander's bad side. And he would have been right.

There is always a certain degree of tension between the appearance you wish to convey and the truth of the situation. I clearly chose to remain true to myself. As far as I was concerned, there was no place for make believe. There were other ways to change the way people saw me.

INVITATION

There are various quarters on board navy ships. There were rooms where we had our meals, where we watched movies at night and where we had parties on the weekends while we were in port. These are like the living room of the ship. There also are sailors' quarters, corporals' quarters and petty officers' quarters and officers' quarters – '*the long room.*' The commander had his own accommodation – 'the cabin'. This is where he sleeps and eats, but it's also his living room. The rooms are separated so as to create some sort of professional distance, but also to prevent men from having to be in the same room with their superior officers all the time and to enable them to blow off some steam, when necessary and possibly engage in conversation with like-minded persons. They are welcome in other rooms of course, however only if invited. The commander is the only one left to himself.

'Can I have another beer?' I asked the colleague behind the bar. We had moored in Belfast a couple of hours ago and the bar in the long room had been opened. The other officers were all there enjoying a pint. It was obvious that the department heads were about to disembark, all dressed and ready to go. The mood in the long room was pretty good, the music was turned up and the beer was flowing freely when the commander entered the long room. He didn't knock and came in with an air as if to say, 'Here I am.' He looked at his baby duck department heads and gave a satisfied nod. Then he walked up to the bar. *'Can I have a beer?'* the commander asked, looking quite pleased to finally be in a foreign port again. *'Who invited you commander?'* I blurted out, obviously not considering a possible loss of face. He looked at me and the colleague behind the bar held the glass against the tap, but waited to pull the lever. It was as if the entire world stood still for a moment. It was quite apparent that there was no love lost between us and everybody on board was aware of this. 'This is MY ship, MY SHIP,' I saw him thinking, but regaining his composure just in time, he said: *'The First Officer gave me permission to enter, we will be off soon.'* The tap was finally pulled and the commander was handed a cold beer. He turned around, emptied his glass and took his baby ducks with him for their usual rental car routine. *'Ouch,'* my colleague behind the bar said to me, *'that was a bit of an awkward situation.'*

I had really behaved poorly and I knew that it had not been a very smart thing to do. This old-school commander would not take this lightly. It meant a loss of face for the commander and myself and a lack of resilience on my part. I had not been very diplomatic, more like a bull in a china shop. I had done exactly what I should not have done, despite the fact that I had remained very polite and that it really wasn't anything to get excited about. Sometimes a situation is so sensitive that it requires more than merely abiding by the rules. What purpose did it serve, asking him a question like that? After all, there were at least twelve other officers present in the long room. But the damage had been done and the relations were on edge again. I had to realize that I was the one on the wrong side of the situation. A couple of moments later, the commander's departure was announced over the ship's PA-system.

This expression of my frustration was not the most diplomatic move I ever made, nor was it the smartest. I had been trying to get some recognition of my work for a very long time, without any result. I had not realized that the minor elements in a process also contribute to the end result. It reminded me of the time when I had tried to get a golf course qualification and I really should've learned from that experience. All I was thinking about was my end goal and I had failed to consider the importance of the process. Unfortunately, it seems that the process is often more important than the result.

THE PROCESS OR THE RESULT?

Achieving the objective is the most important thing. Preferably in the fastest way possible. So, when I started playing golf, I had but one goal: to get that course qualification as soon as possible. Following an intensive weekend course, I was ready for it. There was a theoretical exam on Monday afternoon and if I passed that, I could continue with the practical exam. The theoretical exam was not the most difficult one I had ever taken, so fortunately, I could move on to the golf course after an hour. Things went reasonably well for two holes. Then came the third hole and my golf ball ended up at about 3 ft. from a 7-foot wide ditch. The green was behind the ditch so, basically, I needed to hit the ball about 100 ft. to get it near the flag. But no. On the first attempt, the ball dribbled into the water. The examiner stood behind me and scribbled something in his notebook. 'No problem,' I thought, as I picked a new ball from my bag and dropped it on the spot where the first one had been. I took my position, squeezed the club a little firmer and swung it, only to watch the second ball drop into the water after the first one. I gave the examiner an embarrassed look and apologized with a sheepish smile.

I went back to my bag and took out a third ball, dropped it on the same spot and repeated my swing. This time, not only did the ball go into the water, but also a big clump of grass. Frustrated as I was, I had apparently 'decided' to send my third ball to the bottom of the ditch along with the clump of grass. My face turned red and I was fuming. At that moment, the examiner said to me '*Jochen, just grab a ball, walk to the other side of the water and drop the ball there.*' I slowly turned and looked at the instructor, slightly irritated and I thought, 'Over my dead body. I get my ball across the water.' I swallowed twice, dropped my eyes and calmly said to him, '*I'll get it across from this side, don't you worry.*' But the damage had been done and I was really angry inside. 'Why won't that ball go across!?' By the time I gave up the battle, I had lost seven more balls to the water. I had been beaten by a stupid 7 foot ditch. I had one more hole to go and only two balls left. The result was that I flunked my practical exam for 'golf ability.'

My golf disaster was a good moment to reflect on during this failure. What had been the main cause of my lost battle with the ditch? In this instance, the game of golf offers an interesting lesson for a future leader. And I'm not talking about my stubborn refusal to walk to the other side to hit the ball. No, this is about a process. The trick to golf is not to think about the result. If you start to think about how the ball will roll into the hole or bounce onto the green while you're in the middle of your swing, it will go wrong. The key to the process is in the details. Only when you carry out the process perfectly and don't think of the result will you see the ball flying through the air. There is no need to apply force or to look up too quickly to see if the ball is going in the right direction. The process of carrying out your golf swing calmly will automatically produce the desired result. Then you can start working on this process. In which area can you improve your swing? Which detail of the swing needs adjusting in order to improve the result? Your grip, the position of your feet, the posture, the back swing, your head, shoulders, the blade of your club, your weight distribution, your follow-through are all the aspects that influence your results. With golf, you cannot work on the result directly, you need to adjust the process. Golf is a bit of an extreme example here, because only thinking of the result will produce a negative influence here. Yet there is a lesson to be learned here for the future leader. If you constantly think about the results, without considering how you got to the point where you are, it will go wrong. The leader focuses primarily on the process and only uses the result to adjust the process. If, after a beautiful swing, the ball ends up way off course, you will have to adjust the process. It is the same thing for a leader. Good results do not always mean something. How did you achieve these good results? What does your team think about the way you achieved them? Are the results a direct consequence of your magnificent leadership, or do people actually find you a bad leader? Does nobody want to work for you or is the executive director the driving force behind the good results? These are important considerations for a leader. You will need to be aware of the process. The process is at least as important as the result. The leader has control over the process. There are plenty of others who will hold you accountable for the result. You can bet on that.

> **Building blocks of leadership:**
> *Self-knowledge, situational awareness*

A GOOD MORNING

'*Good morning commander, it is six o'clock. Time to wake up. The weather outside is excellent, sunny and clear, but still a bit nippy. A boat transfer was scheduled for this morning, but this has been cancelled. No other particulars to report sir,*' I said cheerfully through the phone. '*Okay, thanks,*' I heard the sleepy voice say on the other end of the line. This week I had the Morning Watch and the Dog Watch, from 04.00 to 08.00 hours and from 16.00 to 20.00 hours, respectively. Twice a day I was on watch on the bridge with all of the drills that are held during these hours. The person who had the Morning Watch had standard orders to call the commander and wake him up, immediately informing him of any particulars from the night before or about the day ahead. After forty-five minutes, I saw an Ajax mug making its way up the staircase to the bridge. '*Good morning commander,*' I said cheerfully. He sort of nodded in my direction and stuck his nose into some nautical charts. '*Any particulars to report, officer of the watch?*' he asked me. '*No sir, nothing other than what I told you earlier on the phone commander,*' I responded brightly again. I had been awake for hours, after all. '*DAMMIT!*' he shouted, '*How about the boat transfer that has been cancelled!!! Don't you think I should know that!?*' He roared across the bridge. My mouth fell open in astonishment. '*Commander, that was one of the first things I said to you when I gave you a wake-up call this morning,*' I said in an innocent and astounded voice. '*WHAT? You never told me that!*' His gaze went straight through me. It was quite clear that he was convinced that I had not told him and that he had been forced to find out for himself. Ranting furiously, he walked off the bridge. Well, that was a great start of the day.

LAMBASTING OR COACHING

I simply could not develop a good relationship with the commander. Maarten was not the kind of person to provide any counter-balance and the other department heads thought better of it than to raise any objections.

The source of all this misunderstanding was that in the commander's mind, I did not live up to his standard. This was possibly caused by conflicting personalities and the fact that he was absolutely convinced that there was only one way of leading and that was his way. As a leader, you will need to realize that you fail if your people don't succeed. How can you get the best out of your people? By screaming across the ship's bridge? By completely belittling them and lambasting them *in front of everybody*?

Over time, people develop unique personalities that reflect their personal wishes for their life's journey. This also shapes the relationship that you, as a leader, have with others. You project your wishes on others and you anticipate, based on your expectations of how others may react. Subsequently, you do not respond to their actual reaction, but to the manner in which you perceive it. The use of a certain dominant style (tyrannical behavior, micro-management, inaccessibility or conflict-avoidance) is often deeply rooted in personality style and can cause conflicts for a leader[13]. As a leader, you will need to be aware of this and adjust your dominant style in such a way as to invest more into coaching and guiding your people. Show that you have faith in them and stimulate them to perform even better. What is it you actually expect from your people? It is perfectly all right to set the bar high. Very high, even. After all, doesn't this also determine the boundaries by which you operate?

As a leader, you will hopefully delegate certain tasks to your people. You may have to confront certain people if their progress is not in accordance with your wishes. Either way, you will have a choice. You will have multiple choices and options to ensure proper functioning of the team and its members. This requires leaders with good judgment of character, leaders who are able to take advantage of all visible and invisible competences. This requires leaders who do not only shout

---

[13] M.F.R. Kets - *Wat leiders drijft; een klinische benadering van gedragsverandering in organisaties*; about what drives leaders - a clinical approach to behavioural change in organisations; Uitgeverij Nieuwezijds, Amsterdam, 2007

and scream, but adaptive leaders who can adjust to the circumstances and to the people. Effective leaders display complex behavior and may assume different, sometimes contradicting roles.[14] The flexibility of the leader and the ability to handle the leadership styles, perhaps even determines his success...

> **Building blocks of leadership:**
> *Demanding, judge of character, adaptive*

THE LAST STRAW

I noticed that it became increasingly difficult for me to get over certain disputes with the commanding officer. The confrontations increased in number and in my view, they became more and more unreasonable, but each time, I tried to make more of an effort. I tried to gain sympathy, but above all, I tried to perform well. I only focused on the result. When I went to bed at night, as tired as I was, I would still go through the notes I had made. Mine was the bottom half of a bunk bed and I had scribbled countless calculation rules on the underside of the mattress above me. This way, I went to sleep looking at them and I woke up looking at them. Every time, I thought, 'You will not get me down'. Every day, I hoped for the relationship to improve and I always tried to do well. Maybe I was trying too hard to put in a proper performance, causing me to run faster than I should have. I had been on board this vessel for almost a year and the situation still had not gotten any better. However, outside the harbor of Den Helder, I got a new opportunity to prove what I was capable of while at sea.

'*Attention, this is the bridge,*' I hailed my orders over the ship's PA-system. I had made good progress with the checklist of the assigned task. I walked over to both bridge wings to verify whether there was any sea traffic near us or perhaps behind us, which might pose a danger for our next maneuver. A small vessel was to come alongside us to drop off two men. Obviously, the small vessel had to be maneuvered out of the wind

---

[14] R.E. Quinn – *Een kader voor managementvaardigheden*; a management briefing providing a framework for management skills; Academic service, The Hague, 1998

so as to enable the men to get on board easily. I gave my instructions to the helmsman, who repeated the instructions as he complied. At that moment, a loud roar came from the starboard bridge wing. '*DAMMIT, GET OVER HERE!!! Look outside before making the turn. Look behind you, dammit. LOOK!*' he pointed, stamping his foot in rage. His face had turned red. There were about eight others present on the bridge wing and all conversations had ceased. All that could be heard on the bridge wing and on the bridge itself was the outburst of anger directed at me. At that moment, something inside me snapped. I crossed the high threshold to the bridge wing, intending to punch the commander in the face so hard that he would fly up thirty feet in the air and land in the water, ninety feet below. I saw the bystanders looking at me, shocked by the anger in my eyes and the determination in my step. The time it took for me to get from the bridge to the wing was probably exactly the same amount of time that I needed to regain my senses. The look in the commander's eyes showed me that he had not expected this. I managed to get ahold of myself and instead of punching him, I just yelled at him that I damned well had looked and that he would have seen this, if he hadn't been bleating like an old crone on the bridge wing. '*Otherwise, do it yourself,*' I said, about ten inches from his face. I turned around, having no idea what was going on around me anymore. The small vessel had come alongside. Pulling the binoculars over my head, I placed them on the chart table and walked off the bridge with a sense of relief. Maarten accompanied me to the long room and we both dropped down on the couch. We just sat there for a few moments, without speaking. Eventually, Maarten got up and poured two cups of coffee. He was clearly just as overwhelmed by the situation as I was. '*I really don't understand what happened just now,*' Maarten said, with an innocent look in his eyes. 'Coward,' I thought to myself, but I decided against saying it. It was obvious that Maarten was genuinely shaken up by the situation. '*Oh well, what's done is done,*' I said. By then, I had completely calmed down and I had no regrets whatsoever.

STICK UP FOR YOUR PEOPLE

If you are the leader of a group of people, then you must take responsibility for them. These are your people! This is how you should feel and what you should emanate at all times. Your people should know you are there for them and in turn, they will be there for you when needed. Maarten was not that kind of leader. He was more afraid of the commander than anyone else was. As my direct manager, he absolutely failed to have my back at the times when it mattered most. Sure, it is nice that he thinks that everything is going well and that he doesn't understand the commander's behavior either, however, that doesn't do anyone any good. The people for whom you would go through fire and water, are the ones who will decisively and bravely stand behind you in times of hardship.

If the big boss makes unjustified remarks about how one of your staff members performs, this staff member will expect you, as his immediate superior, to talk to the big boss behind closed doors and explain to him that this is not justified. If you don't do this or if you can't do this, then you should ask yourself whether or not you are suited for a leadership role. There are various ways to address such a matter, of course. As a leader, you will need to know exactly how to get this message across people who are both higher and lower in rank.

If I could have blindly trusted my immediate superior to stick up for me, I probably would have swallowed such severe snubbing in this situation as well. After all, I would have known that Maarten had my back and it would not have been up to me to tell the commander that he had been wrong and that I had actually followed the correct procedure. Leadership is about also showing courage and decisiveness and always being there for your people. The leader, in both his words and actions, shows that he supports his case and his people!

> **Building blocks of leadership:**
> *Responsibility, decisive, courage*

SAYING FAREWELL

A few moments later, the First Officer entered the long room and asked me to come see the commander. '*Shall I go with you?*' Maarten asked. I noticed that I had become indifferent and told him that it didn't matter to me either way. Actually, it was a great relief that I had finally spoken my mind instead of taking all that pent up frustration with me to my cabin. Maarten and I walked up the narrow stairs towards the cabin together and in my mind, I had promised myself not to allow the commander to act superior any longer. What little respect I had left for the man had disappeared into thin air. I entered without knocking and said, '*I was summoned.*' Behind me, I heard Maarten say, '*Good afternoon commander.*' Nobody reacted to this. From the corner of my eye, I saw the First Officer seated at the long table in the same place where I had sat when I'd first met the commander. That was a year ago. '*Yes Jochen,*' the commander said, calmly leaning back in his chair. '*Actually, I don't know what is going on. Why can't we see eye to eye?*' I could sense him pretending to ponder this question, only to then tell me that he wanted me to leave. Before he was able to finish his sentence, I said, '*Oh, but I know the answer to that one, really. I think that you are a bad leader. You have no clue whatsoever how to get the best out of people. Our collaboration has become a complete failure and your lack of leadership is largely responsible for this.*'

The tension caused my voice to become somewhat distorted. Subconsciously, I knew I was signing my death sentence. The commander was taken aback by my straightforward approach for a moment. He had to think twice before reacting. After more than a year of being bullied, more than a year of pulling out all the stops without any recognition whatsoever, these two seconds felt like a great victory to me. '*Well, then I see no reason for us to continue working together and I think it would be better for you to leave this ship,*' he said, after he had regained his composure. '*Fine,*' I responded and without awaiting any reaction, I turned around and walked out of the cabin.

PUT YOURSELF IN SOMEONE ELSE'S SHOES
After this terrible experience with the ship's commander, I looked at myself and asked, 'Where could I have done things differently? Where should I have done things differently?' One of the things I could blame myself for was the fact that I hadn't been able to maintain my composure, so as to bend the situation to suit my needs. I had thrown all diplomacy overboard. I had failed to empathize with the mindset, the motives and the emotions of the commander. I was also unable to create the right environment for the commander and myself to get in line with each other, nor had I been able to instill sufficient courage in Maarten, which he needed to stand up for me. In short, I was lacking a great many necessary skills.

Therefore, if you then decide to enter into the discussion or pick up the battle axe, you will need to think about the goal you are trying to achieve. What are you are prepared to do to meet this goal and what are you not prepared to do? In particular, you need to ask yourself the question, 'How do I gain support for my opinion?' Creating a support base is part of 'managing up' - directing people with higher authority. This may be your boss, or possibly the person who makes the final decisions. In every conversation, you need to ensure that not only you come out ahead, but also that your conversation partner benefits as well.[15] In this conversation, you will need to be aware of the concept 'face'.[16] 'Face' is a synonym for the loss of face. Face is a matter of balance. As soon as the balance is under threat of disruption, the face of the participants will be in jeopardy. All of the members of a conversation must try to preserve the face of the other members. This is done in many ways, including providing signs at appropriate moments during the conversation, showing that they appreciate and respect the others and take them seriously. Depending on the hierarchical relations of this conversation, you may need to pay more attention to this. In the end, it is all about building support for your opinion, plan or objective.

A coaching course may help. Here you will learn how to listen and to ask the right questions.[17] Learn to coach people to a better result, a different way of communicating or a better way of leading. I am convinced that with this knowledge, I would have been able to prevent the conflict with the commander. In every conflict situation, there are only losers. A real leader is able to control such a situation. If you have the capacity to strike exactly the right chord with the people above and below you in the hierarchy, you will be able to maintain a workable situation. The future leader must also be able to maintain control over himself in all sorts of situations. He must be able to produce exactly the right skill to be able to see eye to eye with everybody. He must be adaptive. He cannot be simply a social or authoritarian leader who isn't open to reason.

---

[15] M.S. Dobson, D. Singer Dobson - Managing up; 59 ways to build a career-advancing relationship with your boss, AMACOM, New York, 2000

[16] S. Gerritsen - *Een goed gesprek; over communicatieve vaardigheden*; about communicative skills; Uitgeverij Nieuwezijds; Amsterdam, 2001

[17] L. Cauffman - *Oplossingsgericht management & coaching; simpel werkt het best*; about solution-oriented management and coaching keeping it simple works best; Uitgeverij Lemma, Utrecht, 2005

Years later, when I was able to objectively reflect on the time I spent on that ship, it became clear that I had learned a lot from this. The situation would have turned out to be so much different had I understood that I was also part of the process and that I could have adjusted the situation myself. If I had known that, I would have been able to be more resilient. At least two people are involved in every conflict situation and at least two people will also be at fault.

In any case, the commander of the ship caused me to develop a critical, highly demanding view. In order to do a good job, I started walking on eggshells and was constantly on alert. I would think out in advance how to answer every possible critical question. I became critical of my work and myself.

It also occurred to me that perception is important and that an individual can influence this, both positively and negatively. No matter how hard you try, if your image shows that you never do more than the bare minimum, you're fighting a losing battle. You only have one chance to make a first impression.

Finally, you're not given command over a marine vessel out of the blue. There are many years of dedication and hard work in this. A leader has earned the benefit of the doubt through the number of positions a man has held and the experience that he has generated. After all, there are only a few people who are allowed to lead a platform that was created to be deployed in the most extreme situations. A leader of such a unit deserves more credit than I gave him as a young officer.

Building blocks of leadership:
Resilience, demanding

4. UNDER WATER

Example is not the main thing in influencing others.
It is the only thing. - Albert Schweitzer - (1875 - 1965)

I had made myself a promise never again to spend so much time doing work that I did not enjoy, so I put in a request to become a diving officer. In the diving course, rank is irrelevant. It is impossible to learn to dive if there is a hierarchy in place between trainees and instructors. It was twelve months of really rolling up your sleeves and it was clear from the beginning that in the world of divers, actions speak louder than words. Entering the course as an officer puts you at a disadvantage from the start, as you will have to prove you have the right stuff and that you are not just a paper pusher who spends his days sitting behind a desk. This is a world of tough guys and dangerous work, where other features of the leader are emphasized. Fortunately, many features are universal.

DIVER'S ASSESSMENT
In order to be eligible for the diving course, a thorough assessment was required yet again. This assessment consisted of a conversation with a psychologist, a fitness assessment in the pool and a medical examination at the Royal Navy's diving medical center in Den Helder. I had a full physical there, including an ECG, and blood and urine tests, but particular attention was paid to the lungs. Fortunately, I passed these medical assessments easily, even if the lung tests were a bit unpleasant. Apart from all the different lung tests, there is a test in the swimming pool, which is the great stumbling block for many who aspire to become a diver. The swimming test normally requires some practice time, but as was so often the case - many times unjustly so - I thought that practicing was for those without talent. So there I was on this cold Thursday morning, having had no training, in front of the Den Helder municipal swimming pool.

'*Good afternoon gentlemen and lady,*' a young petty-officer greeted us. '*My name is sergeant Pieter and today we will enter the final phase of the diving assessment.'* I looked around at the others and saw some pretty fit looking marines in our group. I secretly started to feel sorry that I hadn't prepared better, but it was too late to be sorry now. Sergeant Pieter gave a brief explanation about the general rules in the swimming pool and before I knew it, I was in the water, following the person in front of me. *'Piece of cake,'* I thought. We had to swim a couple of warm-up laps at an easy pace and then the swimming test began. Four laps of freestyle, two laps backstroke. Then four laps freestyle and also two laps backstroke, only now with over thirteen pounds of lead tied around your waist.

During the instructions, we were told that as soon as we had to grab onto the edges of the pool, we would immediately have to get out and that would be the end of the line for us as far as the diving course was concerned. This was a kind of test of character, as grabbing the edge would equal failure. After swimming, we were expected to tread water for two minutes, without touching the edges. Subsequently, we had to take the weight belt off and drop it to the bottom, then dive down to retrieve it. When we reached the belt at the bottom, we had to put it back on and swim up to the surface again.

Considering all the training many of my fellow course members had already undergone, I was becoming increasingly worried. The impressive entourage didn't really help either. Standing next to the pool were a doctor, a psychologist and two dive leaders, while two divers observed us in the water. I told myself firmly that whatever happened, I would not touch the edge. *'Good luck gentlemen. You may start.'* resonated through the swimming pool. I started on my laps, thinking about how nice the breaststroke was. After six laps, I was handed a weight belt again and things started to get more difficult, but I managed fairly well. 'Don't celebrate just yet,' I said to myself, 'all those people are not standing there observing us for nothing.'

As soon as I had finished my six laps, I immediately had to start treading water. So there we were, all the trainees, treading water, our fingers held up above the water. This is when I realized that the forward motion of swimming was what had kept me afloat. I sank a bit below the surface and had a hard time staying up. *'Two minutes!'* someone shouted to me from the side. Two minutes? I had only been at it for five seconds, for crying out loud. Okay Jochen, hold on. There was this huge analog clock above the pool with a second hand, which I could see slowly ticking away. I was already sensing a cramp rising in my legs. I started to breathe a little harder and hoped I wouldn't swallow any water while trying to keep my head above water. Darn, time was going so slow … only twenty-five seconds gone, twenty-six, twenty-seven … From the corner of my eye, I could see my fellow trainee Walter treading water and I realized how important proper preparations were.

In the morning, when we were waiting in front of the pool, Walter had told me how he had practiced twice a week, swimming and treading water with the lead weights tied around him. Therefore, while I was huffing and puffing for the entire pool to hear, Walter was up out of the water, far above his waist, two fingers in the air. I was sure he would start humming a tune any minute, while I was almost drowning next to him after just thirty-five seconds … thirty-six, thirty-seven, thirty-eight … 'Come on Jochen, two minutes is nothing,' I thought to myself, but I couldn't keep my eyes off the clock and that thing was going so terribly slowly. '*One more minute!*' I heard from the side. From here it's just a count-down, come on, you're passed the halfway point,' I encouraged myself. To put some more pressure on myself, I slowly moved backward, away from the edge. Tock! I ran right into one of the lane dividers installed between the lanes and I could feel one of the floats in my neck. For a brief moment, my head was supported ever so slightly by this long cord with floats. It was an enormous relief. '*Come over here!*' sergeant Pieter shouted from the side. As if nothing had happened, I continued to tread water and let myself drift away from the lane divider again. That instant of good fortune, that tiny moment of relief, they could never take away from me. 'Thirty more seconds,' I thought, 'we're going to make it, for sure.' '*Fingers above water, Hekker,*' I heard from the side again. Words were meaningless at this point. Chortling and huffing and puffing, I continued to tread water, trying to keep my head, or actually just the edges of my mouth, the tips of my lips, above water. My heart felt like it was pounding its way out of my chest and my breathing rate must have been eyeing a spot in the *Guinness Book of Records*. Ten more seconds and I lowered one of my arms to the clip of the lead belt. The sergeant looked at his stopwatch, he looked at me, and I looked at the analog clock. 'Time dammit, TIME,' I thought and a split-second later I heard, '*Two minutes!*' The words were barely out of his mouth and my lead weights were at the bottom of the pool. '*Diver Hekker, hurry up, go after it!*' I took two more deep breaths and with a duck dive, I went after my weight belt. When I got down to it, I set it straight first, stepped over it and simply tied it around my waist. This is where my experience as a diving hobbyist came in handy. From the corner of my eye, I could see two men treading water on the surface, but without weight belts. I swam up and gave the 'okay' sign. *'Great, you can come out now,'* the sergeant said. I swam to the ladder of the pool and just as I was about to push myself up out of the water, a cramp shot through my left leg. As if pre-arranged, a second later I felt the same pang shooting through my right leg as well. 'At least this didn't happen thirty seconds ago,' I thought to myself. *'Well Hekker, don't ask me how, but you passed this one,'* the sergeant said with a big smile. *'I'd advise you to work on your swimming skills in the months between now and the beginning of your diving course.'* Having come to that conclusion myself already, I responded: *'Thank you sergeant.'*

TO GIVE UP IS NOT AN OPTION
The instructions for the swimming test are simple, 'Grab the edge of the pool and there ends your diving assessment.' The purpose of this is to separate the wheat from the chaff. What good is it, to have someone who cannot persevere? Someone who won't dive because it's too cold? Or someone who comes to the surface, but hasn't finished his task down below? The diving course is a mental and physical test of strength. You also need a certain degree of luck and you cannot fall ill. Inability to dive, for instance as a result of a cold, will mean the end of your diving course. You can help yourself out by taking good care of yourself, wearing warm clothes, eating healthy food and sleeping well.

The diver has certain features that may also be expected of a leader such as the determination to finish a job and constant consciousness of how dangerous it is under water. As soon as you become stressed under water, your ability to make good decisions will be affected. Stress under water is therefore the worst thing that can happen to a diver. The same applies to a leader. Even when you know things can go wrong, you must still find a way to remain calm, to think, to maintain perspective and to make the right decisions.

Building blocks of leadership:
Perseverance, calm, situational awareness

IN THE MUD

'Ready? Okay, descend!' I opened the outlet valve of my dry suit, pressed the air out of it, blew the air out of my lungs and slowly, the world around me went dark. Dark, quiet and cold. The first months of the diving course consisted of spending as much time in the water as possible. And I was so cold. It was okay in the pool, during the first months of the course. The emphasis there was on mastering certain routines. Now, after two weeks as 'Trainee Divers' we had to get into the Den Helder port for the real thing. In January, this can be a rather chilly affair.

I knew that the spot where I was diving was thirteen to seventeen feet deep. The strange thing was that I couldn't feel the bottom. As I learned later, the bottom was one enormous muddy surface that you gradually disappear into. Dirty, stinking sludge. As soon as you got out of the water again, you had this odor on you from the filthy, stinking mud. You could rub and scrub in the shower all you wanted, but you just could not get rid of that smell. It got into your pores, under your nails, behind and in your ears, everywhere. The first time I went into open water, I disappeared into the mud. After a few moments, I thought that I should have reached the bottom. I felt around for the signaling rope I had tied around my waist and pulled it. One pull means you have reached the bottom. I felt one pull back, meaning they understood. Then I gave another pull meaning everything was okay. So there I was in the mud, in the port of Den Helder, blowing bubbles. It was freezing cold; this was January, after all. But it was so peaceful. All that I heard was the sound of my own breathing and the flow of air bubbles going up to the surface. The first thing you think about are the routines. Is the signaling rope free? Did I close the outlet valve of my dry suit? Which sign should I receive? How long will they leave me down here? What sort of animals live down here? In the distance, there is the sound of ships sailing through the port. And slowly, but surely, your thoughts start drifting away.

Until the cold starts to get to you. The first uncontrollable shivers overwhelmed me. Right then, I got the sign one with four, one pull on the rope around my waist, then my response with one pull back. Then I got four pulls, meaning I had to go up to the surface. I prepared myself and gave four pulls back meaning the diver is coming up. I slowly started to go up. I had opened my outlet valve and slowly followed the shot line to ascend. The great dark world was gradually becoming lighter.

In no time, through the last couple of inches of water, I could see my classmates watching and smiling at me from the quay. Once I reached the surface, I gave the okay-sign. 'You can get out, diver Hekker,' the instructor said. I stepped onto the quay and started shivering from the cold. My lips turned purple and I couldn't feel the rest of my body. Later on, I learned that having a bit more airflow through your suit provides better insulation and you'll be able to withstand the cold a bit better. I really wished I had known that earlier.

'F' FOR FAIL: AN 'F'!!

After weeks of 'working under water', we bid farewell to those who only took the short course. For the ship's divers, this was the end of the line. Their work in the navy would not go beyond inspections under the ship and some light tasks at a depth of about fifty feet. The 'frogmen' of the Dutch marine corps were destined to further specialize in the so-called 'attack dives.' However, the majority of our class went all the way to become a clearance diver, meaning that we first spent a couple of months on the mine action module (which focused on clearing mines) and then the general diver's module which also included salvage diving. In this part of the course, we went diving with a system where the air supply came through a long hose from the surface, all the way to the diver. The equipment for this 'surface-supplied diving' is used under difficult circumstances, so in principle, the air supply is unlimited.

'Men, on Monday morning, we will go diving in Den Oever,' our new dive leader shouted across the rafts. Major Ad was a real old-school diving master. The tougher, the better. The major favored curse words that referred to the female gender when trying to make a point. Women themselves were of little to no use and, on top of that, he was always right. Nevertheless, I felt some sympathy for him from the start. It was all too obvious that diving in general, but especially the culture within the diving community, meant everything to him. He actually thought it was ridiculous that we were allowed to use gloves in winter. In the past, gloves were not permitted. The major looked sharp. A real old-fashioned soldier, as if he came straight off the set of a Hollywood movie. Crew cut, shiny shoes, all the decorations depicting him as a diver prominently on display on his uniform. He always spoke in short bursts, always in a loud voice, never issued so much as a compliment. The only way that you knew you had done well was if he hadn't mercilessly chastised you.

That weekend proved to be one of the coldest in decades. Temperatures had not risen above freezing all weekend. It was so cold that in the province of Friesland, they were already discussing the famous Dutch ice-skating tour of eleven cities, a 175-mile outdoor skating marathon across canals and ponds, which was only held when it was extremely cold. All I could think about was the freezing waters that I would be sitting in during the coming week.

We would not be diving in the port of Den Helder this week, but instead off of a moving dive support vessel, which was waiting in the harbor of the small town of Den Oever. *'Men, this will be the week of deep drift diving,'* the major shouted from the passenger seat, on the way to Den Oever. The major always referred to us as boys or men, despite the fact that we also had a female trainee diving officer in our group. *'Time to separate the men from the boys,'* he continued, followed by a claim that back in the day, there was no limit. *'Dive until you drop, is what we did. You're lucky that diving is not permitted in currents of more than one knot. I assure you that I will merely be stretching the envelope. One knot!'* We had no idea what that meant, one knot. Is that difficult? Is it tough? Is it easy? I realized that one knot is one nautical mile. That's over 2,000 yards per hour. That meant that if I were to let myself go, after an hour I would surface about 2,000 yards away. Nice to know, but it actually didn't make me any wiser.

The van turned into the parking lot of the Den Oever harbor and there was 'Hydra', our dive support vessel. The first thing we noticed was that Hydra was trapped in ice. Were my eyes playing tricks on me? The harbor was frozen shut! The major decided, however, that we would just have to start diving anyway. He wanted to be sure that we would get the feel of the mixed gas diving system. As if we would've forgotten how it worked over the course of one weekend. He did, however, give us something to remember, because this meant we would first have to break through the ice, before we would be able to dive. So there we were, at almost noon on Monday, 'making bubbles' in the harbor of Den Oever.

Early the next morning, after having spent a night on board the Hydra, it was time to leave the harbor. The Hydra steamed ahead, towards deeper waters. After a short trip in which we passed the time with diving preparations, we were finally ready for our last briefing before going into the water. *'Briefing in the coffee room,'* I heard over the ship's PA and so I headed that direction accompanied by my six remaining classmates.

'*Men,*' the major said, 'It's *finally time for the real thing.*' He gave us an extensive briefing about safety followed by clear instructions about who would do what in case of a general emergency or a diving accident. It seemed to me as if everything had been thought through. '*The first diver is...*' The major looked around, his eyes stopping when they reached mine. I gazed back. '*Hekker,*' the major continued his briefing. '*The current is exactly one knot when you descend. The depth of the water is 11.2 fathoms and I expect you to build a window.*' Building a window was something we had practiced extensively, so this should be no problem, I thought.

Building the window means that you descend with twenty nails and a hammer. Once at the bottom, you ask for a wooden plank, which is then sent down to you. You have an additional rope fastened to your body for this, which they tie the plank to at the surface. Then you reel in the rope to get the plank. The thing about wood is that as soon as you let go of it, it will shoot up to the surface like a rocket, due to its positive buoyancy. So, the trick is to hold on to the plank at all times, while hitting the nails into it. You also have no visibility at the bottom so you have to do everything by touch. In total, you get four planks sent down to you, which you use to build a window. You have to hit five nails into each corner. Four on the edges and one in the middle like five dots on dice. On the surface was where the fun was. Everybody would burst out laughing if the diver let go of his plank and it suddenly popped up to the surface. When you finally got your head above water after the exercise, Major Ad would shout across the decks, '*FAILED! ... An 'F' for Failed!*' I didn't think there were any real consequences attached to this 'F'.

'*Hekker, ready?*' I nodded my head to signal that I was. With a hose in your mouth, your mask on and a continuous flow of air running into your mouth, it's pretty hard to talk. That was the only disadvantage to this mixed gas diving system. When on the surface, all you could do was try to get by, because the system produces a continuous flow of air, even when you don't need it. It's great under water, but on the surface, this is very uncomfortable. Your cheeks blow up with excess air and saliva flows out of your mouth. The major walked around me. He checked that all of the lines of my diving system were properly attached. He checked the carbon dioxide absorption canister to see if it was filled, checked the proper flow settings of the mixed gas and screwed tight the outer cap of the equipment on my back.

I was packed and loaded and ready to go into the water. I had all of this diving gear on my back and a signaling line around my waist. I had my dry suit on, diving cap on my head, mask on, hoses in my mouth, emergency air supply on my upper leg, a knife tied to my lower leg and fins on my shoes, of course. Altogether, I could pass for an astronaut, only unfortunately, there was no weightlessness and I was dressed in black. As soon as I walked down the steps of the vessel and my fins hit the water, I could feel the force of that current. I stood for a moment, focused on my position and made sure that the signaling line in my hand was still running straight up. I used my other hand to grab the descent line, which was attached to the ship. This line was a ship's rope with a 2-inch diameter. One end was attached to the ship and there was a big block of concrete on the other end. The end with the concrete block would easily sink to the bottom and you could use it as a 'table' to carry out the work.

I grabbed the descent line and lowered myself into the water. My body was immediately pulled horizontally by the current. I was like a flag hanging from a flag post in a tropical storm. '*Ready?*' the major called out from the deck. He gave me the OK sign and waited for me to signal 'OK' back. For a split-second I let go of the line, signaled OK and quickly grabbed the line again. '*Descend!*' I heard, and I pulled myself downward, away from the splashing of the boat, away from all the noise above water, looking for the peace and silence under water. Instead of quickly descending, however, I remained right below the surface. I tightly held on to the descent line with my arms and legs, while trying to prevent the signaling line around my waist from being tangled. After all, this might seriously disrupt my task of constructing a window. I had not even been under water for a minute and I could already feel the acidification of the muscles of my arms beginning. The strong current was literally pulling at my entire body. On top of this, there was a heavy pull on the hoses of my equipment as well – the hoses that provided me with indispensable oxygen. I bit my mouthpiece a bit harder and 'descended' further. I had no idea what was going on, but I just couldn't get down more than three feet. 'Come on, Jochen, let's go!' I thought to myself and then I felt the concrete block under my feet and I was still right at the surface. The current was so strong that I was floating behind the ship, together with the concrete block beneath me. I wasn't going to reach the bottom and I had already reached the end of my descent line.

I pulled the signaling line to indicate that I 'had reached the bottom and everything was okay.' Hopeless! I felt no response on my line, which I figured had curled itself around the descent line a hundred times by now. Okay, so now what? I pulled the line harder this time. Again, nothing. My arm muscles were giving up on me. Sixty-five feet deep, so sixty-five feet of descent line. How on earth was I going to get back? At that point, I decided to start working my way back. It was obvious that as soon as I let go of the line, the current would drag me away. I imagined the scene, me with the hose out of my mouth, no more air supply and my friends having to pull me back on board in this strong current, using the thin signaling line. No, that was not going to happen. In my head, I screamed myself onward. 'COME ON, PULL! PULL!!! Bit by bit, I started to move forward. The air hoses were flapping next to my ears, the water forcefully tugging at my body and my gear. After what felt like ages, I raised my head above the surface. This calmed me a little bit, since I could now be assured of air. With my strength ebbing away, I pulled myself towards the ladder of the ship. This was also extremely difficult. I struggled but continued to pull myself towards the steps. One knot? Not a chance. Even without a frame of reference, I knew this was much more than one knot. It was impossible for people to work under these circumstances. If I could only get my knees onto the bottom step, I thought to myself. This was a fight against the elements. Either I'd get my legs on that ladder, or I would find myself in the water many yards behind the ship in no time. With one final effort, I managed to get one knee on the bottom step and was finally able to relax my arm muscles a bit. I knew that I couldn't have made the decision to return to the ship any later than I did. My heart was beating in my throat like a steam train trying to run through a brick wall. My hands were cramped, my lower arms were numb and my legs were totally done for.

'Everything okay?' the major shouted at me, visibly worried this time. I gave him the OK-sign by forming an 'O' with my thumb and index finger. I climbed further up the ladder and eventually managed to drop my fins on the deck of the Hydra. My classmates removed my diving gear and I literally dropped down on one of the hatches of the rear deck, totally spent. My breathing was still triple the speed that it should have been. The major was looking at me from a distance. He walked over to me and said, '*Hekker! An F!*' and walked off with a big smile on his face. Despite my total exhaustion, I could not stop myself from smiling. We understood each other. It was quite obvious that I had passed his test of competence. After this, diving was suspended because of the heavy current. The rest of the diving course went by in relative calm. The sun came out a bit more and after the summer holidays; we even had classes about explosives. Finally, after twelve months of training, I received the coveted divers pin and I could call myself a Dive Officer of the Royal Dutch Navy.

A diver with standard gear.

LEADING WHEN THE GOING GETS TOUGH

The biggest challenge in leading diving operations is the risks involved in the tasks to be carried out. Every time a dive leader sends a diver under water, it is 'real life.' Every time somebody sits on top of an explosive device, it is 'real life.' Mistakes are not allowed. As a dive leader, you hardly ever have the chance to influence the operation carried out by the diver down below. You have only limited room to maneuver, and the stress level automatically rises as a result. Not everyone is able to cope with this. This obviously also applies to the moments when you are under water yourself. In this environment, stress is a bad counselor.

Your mind needs to be clear for you to be able to save yourself, even when you are 160 or 170 feet under water.

The dive leader who is observing from the sidelines needs to trust all sorts of factors over which he has no control, including the professionalism of the diver, the reliability of the dive system, and the underwater surroundings. However, these are things you can consider in advance, so as to mitigate the risks as much as possible. A dive leader will proactively seek the answers to whatever questions he has. A dive leader is at least able to paint a picture of how things are faring down below. The diver is expected to show a degree of professionalism, but so are the people on the surface. The dive leader doesn't provide an extensive briefing for nothing. During the briefing and during the dive, there is no room to leave any issues unclear. Everybody knows his task and everybody is aware of the fact that this is serious business.

The dive leader is always pondering 'what-if' scenarios. Diving is a race against the clock. From the moment the diver sticks his head under water, the clock starts running. The stopwatch is pressed and the *what-ifs* have started.

Of course, there are diving accidents. Failed diving equipment, wrong decisions under water or simply bad luck during the execution mean that diving is and always has been a dangerous profession. In these are moments, stress levels sky rocket, but these are also the moments that you have trained for. This is where real leaders distinguish themselves from those who only aspire to be leaders. All eyes will turn to whoever happens to be highest in rank and you will have to deliver. You must put everybody in position and start providing aid. You must make sure to display your leadership and to get the situation under control. These are the moments when you justify your leadership. A tough look and a big mouth will not work in situations like this. This is the time to act.

In other moments, your social skills are more important. In particular, when you are surrounded by tough guys who are forced to face more than their fair share of adversity. For example, when the Ministry of Justice calls on you to help find persons missing at sea. This is an extraordinary experience and stress levels will inevitably rise. As soon as you go under water, you know you may encounter a body.

After recovering the bodies of victims, the dive team always receives counseling. There are professional institutions for that purpose, but in most cases, the group process has proven to be particularly successful for healing. That is to say, gathering the whole team together after the job is completed to have a drink and discuss the events as they happened. In these situations, everyone will openly and honestly express what they thought about the job. There will always be some who require a bit more time to process things and there is always professional help available to them. It is up to the leader to point this out to his people. Counseling and personnel care in the broadest sense is also the task of every leader, even in a world full of tough guys.

It is important that you are able to maintain the presence of a leader when called for. You must be able to consider all of the risks and the controlling measures, gaining insight through knowledge and experience. This way, you can get a grip on the situation. Finally, there is no time to allow yourself to be overcome by a loudmouth. You set the boundaries and in the end, you determine what is going to happen. The team does the work, but remember that all eyes are on you when things go wrong. That is part of the charm of being a leader.

> **Building blocks of leadership:**
> *Responsibility, empathy*

5. CHANGE CAUSES RESISTANCE

There is no change from darkness to light
or from inertia to movement, without emotion
- Carl Gustav Jung

Sometimes a leader is required to act firmly. Especially when he is de-voted to the business and he is worried about certain risks of disruption within the organization; when he is the kind of leader who sticks his neck out to make the organization better. Not every leader has developed all his leadership skills or knows immediately which skills are required in a certain situation. However, even the leader who doesn't excel in all aspects of leadership will be able to compensate for this to a certain extent. A leader must have the capacity to adapt to all circumstances. He must be able to assess the situation and adjust his leadership skills accordingly. Does the situation require me to be firm and stolid, or are my other skills required?

WARM WELCOME
On the first Monday morning after completing the diving course, I was in the operational hub of the Defense Diving Group. This building was the heart of 'diving operations'. This is where all the equipment related to diving was kept on high storage racks. There were large piles of air hoses, to provide divers with air from the surface, different types of diving apparatuses, welding equipment, crates and pallets filled with gear. The divers were standing in between all these racks stacked with equipment. Gradually, their number increased as more and more divers entered the building from all sides. In the end, some sixty people were standing around the commander.

'Good morning everyone,' the commander said. The men stared ahead stoically, sipping on their coffee every now and then. Most of them had already observed my presence, but they paid no attention to me whatsoever. Everybody knew I'd just finished the diving course and I actually didn't know a whole lot yet. The majority of the men present here this Monday morning were the tough guy type. Fortunately, I knew that type from my training days. My instructor, after all, had been no different. 'Men, hopefully you all enjoyed your leave and your batteries are recharged for a new week. We have a lot on our schedule, but before you hear more about this, I would first like to introduce you to the new Head of the Diving Technical Research Center. Lieutenant Hekker,' the commander said. 'I expect you to bring him up to speed on everything within our organization as soon as possible.' I expected people would look at me now, nod affirmatively and provide a reassuring smile. Anything that might indicate some kind of sympathy. Unfortunately, I got nothing of the sort. Everybody just kept looking at the commander. So there I stood, looking all crisp in my suit and tie with my shined shoes and my new diving pin on my chest. 'Gentlemen, have a good week.' I heard the commander say and the men turned around, walked to the kitchen for a fresh cup of coffee and that was it. Nobody even took the trouble to welcome me to diving operations.

'Come on, let's get to work,' my predecessor André said to me. He took me to his office and started showing me the ropes, explaining the projects currently underway. André started his computer and opened his e-mail. I saw the number of messages that had not been read: 543. 'There must be a lot of work here,' I thought. Later on, I learned that André was too 'busy' with his work activities, which is why he couldn't get round to answering his e-mails.

'*You're in for a wonderful job as Head of the Diving Technical Research Center,*' André said. '*At the moment, there is a technical investigation underway into a diving accident with mixed gas equipment. I would've loved to have finished this myself.*' What followed then was a barrage of technical details about some pin that was sitting at a crooked angle in a diving system and it affected the pressurized air from the cylinder and different mixes had been disproportionally mixed and I had lost him within the first couple of words of this extensive explanation. 'What in the world is this about?' I thought to myself. If this was the work I was in for in the coming years, things did not look very promising. For the sake of appearances, I acted as if I were very interested.

André shared an office with his right-hand man, flag lieutenant Lars. In addition to the two of them, the Diving Technical Research Center consisted of an equipment department and a technical support department. '*What types of research methods do you use, André?* I asked him. He shifted in his seat for a moment and after pondering the question for a while, he explained to me that he and his flag-lieutenant viewed the situation based on Lars' thirty years of diving experience. Using this experience as a guide, they tried to establish a cause. I left it at that, but I secretly started to ponder what my approach would be, after I had been briefed by André. 'The Diving Technical Research Center also conducts research into diving equipment involved in civilian accidents,' André continued. '*For example, a missing diver in the North Sea was found after a couple of days. The justice department wants to determine all possible causes and they will often let the Diving Technical Research Center investigate for them. Most of the time, they will submit a formal request for assistance.*' He showed me a couple of files and technical surveys including copied papers, old typed out investigation reports, printed versions and photographs. I was surprised by this, but I looked at the collection with great interest. I'm sure it must all be in order in terms of content, but it wouldn't hurt to standardize these reports, I thought.

TIME TO THINK

Over five hundred unread e-mail messages. First, I thought André had to be some sort of miracle worker, being able to do so many things at the same time. Working through five hundred e-mail messages at the end of a day was incredible. Nothing, however, could have been further from the truth. André had a continuous backlog of emails dating back several weeks, or even months. He simply could not get his priorities straight, conclude matters or have people think about their problems themselves and find solutions. In fact, André wanted to do things right for everybody, which made every else's problems his responsibility. If someone had a problem, he would go to André first and the problem would end up on his pile. The word 'no' was not in André's vocabulary.

During a workday, you have to organize your available time. This requires a fair bit of organizational talent, whether or not you recognize that talent. Apart from all the work that needs to be done, you are expected to save sufficient time to read and respond to e-mail messages. You also need to make time to talk to your people and to think things over. Take ten minutes per day to sit back and think. Think about whether or not you're doing things right, about which direction you want to go in, about problems, or better yet, about solutions. Think about leadership. In all the busy work schedules that we impose on ourselves and others impose on us, this important aspect is often forgotten. Time management is essential, especially for a leader with too few hours in a day or days in a week. You will have to prioritize and distribute your focus. This includes freeing up time for yourself and your thoughts! Ten minutes per day will give you fifty minutes per week to think about 'strategy', things like 'Am I doing things right and am I doing the right things? How do I lead?' Fifty minutes a week will give you over thirty-three hours per year. Just imagine all the great ideas you could generate, if you were able to think about them for thirty-three hours.

Building blocks of leadership:
Time management, organizational capacity.

TIMING

The following Monday morning was the first time that I had coffee with the entire staff of the Diving Technical Research Center. After our weekly chat with the commander in the big warehouse, we all crammed together in one of the offices. I listened, and every now and then, I would ask a question if I really didn't understand something. By listening, in particular, I soon found out how the mutual relations of the team were, what issues there were within the department and how the team worked. After coffee, I sat with my right-hand man Lars and had him explain to me how he felt things were going at the Diving Method Center, what he would like to have improved on and what my role, but also what his role, looked like. Lars had over thirty years of experience as a technician in the Royal Navy and he was two years from retirement. Lars was handy, extremely detailed, a perfectionist who basically took apart any device that he got his hands on. One of his good friends told a story about how Lars had once bought a new racing motorcycle from a dealer's shop and when they delivered it, he wouldn't take it. The motorcycle had two miles on the odometer. The sales clerk was cursing and screaming, but Lars stuck to his opinion that he had bought a new motorcycle and not one with two miles on it. Apparently, it was policy for the dealer to test the new bikes by riding a couple of rounds on them. In any case, three months later, Lars got his new motorcycle with zero miles on it. The first thing he did when he came home was take the bike apart, to see that the factory hadn't made any mistakes in assembly. He had stripped the brand new bike down to the bare bones, opened up its insides, cylinders, valves, everything.

Lars was a perfectionist with an eye for every minor detail, no matter how small. I was a generalist, result-driven. I was aware that the last twenty minutes of a project, often take up eighty percent of the time, though not necessarily always. It would take some getting used to for the both of us. We decided together, to launch a couple of 'quick win' projects, such as a clear job demarcation, individual talks with personnel by Lars and standardization of the investigation protocols.

These 'quick wins' are interesting, because they don't take up a lot of energy. The level of acceptance for the accompanying changes is usually a bit higher than it is for big change projects. The 'quick wins' you choose make it clear to others what you feel is important, so be sure to choose carefully, but do not lose sight of priorities. It doesn't make sense to push for your 'quick wins' if the entire organization is made to suffer because of them.[18] The 'quick wins' I had in mind were easy to implement, easy to understand and the results were quickly visible. I presume his social character and positive attitude were the reason why there was very little that Lars and I didn't agree on. I also told him that we would complement each other perfectly. The way I looked at it, he was the expert and I would be the one monitoring the process and generating the ideas. He would be the one directing the men down below and I would be making the reports up top. We agreed that in a couple of weeks, I would be sharing some ideas with him and that he would have the room to comment on these based on his expertise and experience. It was obvious that this took some getting used to for Lars. Freedom in his work. Not having anyone looking over his shoulder all the time, but someone who would rely on the output. This may have taken Lars out of his comfort zone for a moment, but he still viewed his new responsibilities in a positive light. He must've seen plenty of leaders come and go over the past thirty years, so he probably thought, 'I'll believe it, when I see it.'

People are quick to form an opinion. About a person, a situation, a way of working. It is something that happens automatically. Sometimes, you have to adapt your opinion after a while because of evolving insight or

---

[18] P.F. Rollin – 42 Rules for Your New Leadership Role, Super Star Press, California, 2011

because the opinion is weighed against the group's point of view. The group's point of view is often enough to change your opinion, without any rational reason. The leader must be aware of the rational reasoning behind a decision at all times. It takes time to let rationale do its work and it takes time to form an opinion or make a right decision. Our decisions are not only influenced by objective information from choices and alternatives, but also by the behavior that we observe in others.[19] It is therefore very sensible to see how things work out first.

No matter how much I was itching to get to work in my capacity as Head of the Diving Method Center, I thought I would gain more by observing it all from a distance first. On the one hand, you could create a certain image in other people's minds if you immediately start working on your tasks. Imagine yourself in a position where you have worked for many years and all of a sudden, a new leader comes along, who in no time thinks he knows better than you do. On the other hand, it is better to adopt a wait-and-see approach, to have more time and gather more information, so you will be able to better substantiate your opinion. It will also give you time to assess the relations better. What does the informal organization look like? What are the dos and don'ts? Who are the followers, who the trendsetters? You can objectively assess the situation, without addressing the group's opinion.

Timing is important, if you wish to get involved and actively start to direct or even to intervene in the process. As a leader, you may be inclined to keep everything under control. Sometimes, just the presence of a leader is sufficient and actual intervention will have a counter-productive effect. By keeping a proper distance and choosing the right moment, you will maintain a broad perspective on the situation, providing an overall awareness of needs.

One of my colleagues tells a story about how he had to lead a military parade of hundreds of soldiers in a funeral parade for the Royal Family. Obviously, this was not a daily task and he wondered how he to get the job done. Early in the morning on the day in question, hundreds of soldiers gathered in the big square on the Navy base in Den Helder. They would practice here first, before the trip to The Hague. The

---

[19] W.L. Tiemeijer, C.A Thomas, H.M. Prast – *De menselijke beslisser; over de psychologie van keuze en gedrag* – about the psychology of choice and behaviour, Amsterdam University Press, Amsterdam, 2009

platoons gradually started to take shape as the platoon leaders tried to place their people in position. On his own, in the middle of the square, stood my colleague, stoically staring ahead, his sabre on the ground in front of him. He said nothing. People started to recognize each other and slowly began to line up. Every now and then someone would step out of line, but a single look from my colleague in the middle of the square was enough to restore order. Then, out of nowhere, he suddenly set everybody in motion. He told me his strategy was to say nothing at all and simply emanate leadership through his mere presence. 'Leadership from the background.' He was vulnerable, on his own, in the middle of the square but his experiment proved a big success.

> **Building blocks of leadership:**
> *Timing, calm*

A MANAGER CONTROLS, A LEADER INSPIRES

Quick wins, objectives, progress meetings, reorganization - all these things sound pretty nice, but what's the use if there is no vision? What's the use of achieving all these things if you don't know which direction you want to go? It is even worse to have a vision, but know that it is impossible to achieve. That leader is a dreamer, someone who knows how to inspire and motivate, as opposed to the leader whom we wish to be or should be.

The inspirational leader has a clear vision, knows in which direction the organization needs to go and inspires people to achieve the joint objectives.[20] In order to inspire, you need passion and enthusiasm. Without passion and enthusiasm, even the most talented leaders will perform their tasks without inspiring anybody in the process. Passion is the catalyst for everything that makes you productive as a leader. Passion is the difference between a leader who simply performs his tasks and a highly productive leader, who knows how to inspire people and gets

---

[20] Prof. Dr. R. H. Flören, S.F. Jansen RA – *Management ondernemerschap – De stille kracht van het familiebedrijf* – about the silent power of the family business, Wolters Kluwer, Deventer, 2010

them to join in his passion.[21]

Where do you wish to go with your people, your department? This is where a leader distinguishes himself from a manager. The manager prefers not to change things. He manages affairs according to a preset standard and prefers to not create a stir. In contrast, the leader has vision and wishes to realize this vision. If this requires changes to be made, changes will be made, regardless of whether or not this creates a stir. The leader displays courage and decisiveness in his realization of the vision. The manager controls while the leader inspires.

> **Building blocks of leadership:**
> *Passion, vision, inspiration*

---

[21] M. Maccoby – Narcissistic Leaders; Who Succeeds and Who Fails, Harvard Business School Press, Boston, 2007

INTEGRITY

'Jochen, you will be the project officer for a search operation in Lake Gooimeer,' the commander said to me. *'The Ministry of Justice is looking for a young woman and her daughter who have been missing for a long time. They are believed to have been left behind by the former husband, somewhere in the vicinity of the lake. We have managed to collect a substantial number of sonar images and it is now up to you to get this job done with twenty men.'* I suspected that this would be a tough mission. A diving vessel was already on its way to the lake. That would be our diving platform for the week. We had adequate facilities and plenty of equipment to last that entire time.

The petty officer drew up the work plan, including risk inventory, costs, number of man-hours and the plan of action. He was also charged with the day-to-day management of the dives. He directed the men and ensured that the job got done. The latter was what he was born to do. Work plans on the other hand, were like occupational hazards for guys like him. My primary task as a diving officer was to take the operational lead if he wanted to dive himself, or if something should go wrong. In that case of a diving accident, you couldn't have enough people at your disposal. In addition, I was involved with all external communication, with the Justice Department or with the press. In the end, I was responsible, but I let the petty officer take the lead on the dives. He was better at it as he had far more experience than I did. We had identified various hotspots with the sonar images and we dove in those places for three days. In the end, everybody was convinced that the persons we were looking for were not in this area of the lake. Job done and everybody went home.

The day after this special assignment, it was all business as usual again and I was calmly working my way through my e-mail messages and reading my investigation reports. That is, until the petty officer came into my office. *'Good morning, sir,'* he said cheerfully. *'Could you please sign here?'* He placed a piece of paper in front of me with all the names of all the persons who had been present at the diving operation. Behind each name was his or her diving time.

Divers are paid for the minutes they actually spend under water. Considering the risks involved with the work, these are very lucrative minutes. I looked at the list in front of me and I saw that each diver had recorded roughly the same number of minutes. *'But sergeant,'* I said, looking up at him, *'these are not the exact diving times.'* The sergeant looked at me a bit dazed and slightly annoyed he said, *'Sir, this is how we always do it here. To keep track every single minute is such an administrative burden. We do the work. We don't sit behind a desk all day and that deserves something extra. Besides, we were in charge as well and we are held accountable when something goes wrong, but don't get paid extra for that. Don't worry about it, sir. This is how things have been done here for years.'* When he spoke those final words, I noticed a slight smile forming around his mouth and I could tell that he was absolutely convinced that this was the case. *'Sergeant,'* I said, *'I'm going to leave this form right here and think about what to do with it.'* The sergeant turned around angrily, mumbled something about this having been done for years, and walked out my office. I realized that if this had indeed been going like this for years, my not signing it would turn me into an instant 'persona non grata' and in my first month.

I discussed the matter with several diving officers and they all said the same thing. *'That's right. It happens, but it used to be even worse. Years ago, people were placed on the diving list that weren't even there. A diving team of five would show up at a diving vessel and they would have some fifteen diving logbooks with them. That doesn't happen anymore. In short, it's not as bad as it could be.'*

It was unbelievable how times had changed, but regardless of the improvement; I refused to be a part of it. The sergeant was furious, but as soon as I asked him to give me a good reason why I should sign the document, he agreed with me. Shortly thereafter, a new commander came, who properly assessed the risk of rounding off diving minutes. From day one, he made integrity his mission.

EXEMPLARY BEHAVIOR
The integrity of the individual leader is displayed, tested and formed by the dilemmas they face. Every choice that is made in a dilemma also informs how you develop as a leader. Once you've hit that slippery slope, it's difficult to slam on the brakes. Dilemmas, however, create real leaders. Real leaders remain standing in the face of a dilemma and by putting their stamp on the outcome; they give direction to their ideals. A leader should regularly question his level of integrity. The moment he feels that something is not right, it is not right. Your integrity is of crucial importance as a leader. You must set an example. Example is

100

better than precept, and a poor example has a lasting effect, with all the bad consequences that accompany it. The powers and responsibilities afforded to you as a leader and the tools you are given to direct and intervene ensures that integrity is an essential quality of a leader.[22] After all, you will then not be able to accuse others of behaving unethically.

I was tempted to sign the form anyway; after all this was the way things were usually done, but what would have been the result for me? Probably some cranky 'good morning' from the petty officer who would think, 'Oh, you really are no better than the rest, are you?' or reassuring words from older fellow diving officers like, 'Don't worry about it, this has been going on for years.' I had a gut feeling that something just wasn't right. This is when of those moments when you must ask yourself if you will be able to look yourself in the mirror if you do this. Will you be setting the right example? The answer is NO! What applies here, of course, is the old adage, 'Practice what you preach'. You will lose all credibility if you take such matters lightly. You will need to be clear and predictable for your people and you achieve this by acting consistently. If you are in doubt in any dilemma, it is best to avoid even the slightest appearance of unethical behavior, as it may create a perception of you as a leader that you will not be able to get rid of easily. You want to avoid any and all wrong perceptions about your integrity.

> **Building blocks of leadership:**
> *Ethical, consistent*

STRAIGHTFORWARD

The new commander, Rekers, was very clear in his opening speech to his staff, all neatly dressed in their blue uniforms, standing at attention in the warehouse. Rekers referred to the 'can-do' mentality, the professionalism of the staff, but he also hinted at the need for some fresh air to be blown into the organization. His words made it clear that certain 'acquired rights' would quickly come undone. All those present knew

---

[22] L. Moratis – *Maatschappelijk Verantwoord Ondernemen; Basisboek MVO*; about Socially Responsible Business Practices, Koninklijke van Gorcum, Assen, 2006

immediately that he was referring to the wrongfully recorded diving minutes. The new commander was a man of few words. He was a big man with a stocky frame, short-cropped hair, a good set of brains and a huge commitment to the organization. In the past two years, the organization had undergone a change, having expanded from 50 to 150 staff. In short, it was quite a challenge that lay ahead for commander Rekers.

In the first couple of weeks, he had to get used to his role. According to the reorganization plan, the idea was for the acting commander to focus on internal operations, while the commander would attend to the strategic operations and external communication. This all sounds very logical and easy to comprehend in theory, but because of his great commitment, you would regularly find him storming and hollering through the corridors while people complained. Rekers was angry about diving suits that were stored improperly, he thought the dressing rooms were not divided correctly; he recorded what time everyone left at the end of the day. In short, he was micro-managing when the idea had been to focus on strategic operations. His grumpy appearance, his hollering and the fact that he was right about what he said caused people to avoid entering into a dialogue with him.

I wondered how I was going to build a good relationship with this new leader, asking myself the question, 'What would I want if I were the commanding officer of this unit?' Would I want people to say, 'Yes sir, amen' or would I want them to support me and reply to me, give comments and help me realize a better product? From the first day on, I decided to opt for the latter.

DIVISION OF TASKS
It is quite tempting to maintain control over everything. After all, many believe they can do the job better themselves. This may be so in some cases, but think of the advantages if you distribute the tasks beforehand. You make people owners of a process, which ensures commitment. The new commander had to get used to his role. Because of his commitment, knowledge, experience and operational view of matters, he had a hard time switching to strategic thinking. If, as a leader, you find it difficult to let go of operational or tactical thinking, you will need to realize that it's somebody else's task to think about this. As a strategic leader, there are plenty of other possibilities for displaying your commitment or placing your operational stamp on the organization.

Besides this, when the 'strategic thinker' starts to busy himself with matters from the work floor, he also influences the perception of the staff. They will ask themselves if there is nothing better for him to do and if he has no faith in the management team. Everybody knows that internal operations should be directed by someone else. These are all realistic questions you trigger as a leader, when you don't take care of with strategic issues yourself or when you can't delegate tasks. Delegation is essential for any leader who wishes to motivate his staff, encourage the leaders beneath him and to foster a healthy perception of himself. After all, every leader has been in the position of those below him as he has built experience. He trusts his people and that is what he displays. This trust will instantly create a different perception among the people and will have a positive effect on the management team.

Building blocks of leadership:
Delegate, trust

THE NEW GENERATION RISES

In the first weeks, Rekers was like a bull in a china shop. He focused more on external operations and less on ad-hoc internal affairs. Anything he didn't like, he would discuss in the management meetings. However, the cultural change that he wanted to take place could only be achieved with resolute intervention. For many years, the management team had been aware that the positive image that the greater organization had of this smaller managerial unit would be immediately destroyed by a single ethical violation. Yet nobody addressed this.

Rekers thought differently about this. He was quite resolute about this from day one. He promised that he would go to the ends of the earth and back for his men, but also that he would crucify them if they betrayed him. This made sense, particularly in a time of cutbacks, ethical violations and media attention. This intended cultural change had to be addressed directly and thoroughly. Diving minutes were paid based on real minutes and preferably in outside waters, not in the diving simulator. Diving is not breathing under water, but actual practice. Working in high pressure situations. Rekers regularly questioned the legitimacy of dives. Why was this diving officer in the water? Doesn't he have any other tasks? Diving officers would be reprimanded if they failed to finish their tasks, while spending a lot of time in the water. Everybody knew he was right, but nobody agreed with him and he was cursed regularly. However, as time went by, I noticed that the younger, more ambitious generation started to side with him.

The older generation, on the other hand, continued to mope and complain. It was so bad, in fact, that it started to annoy the younger generation. Eventually, the young ones were given more responsibilities and were even held in higher regard, purely and solely because their standard of execution and professional knowledge was raised to a higher level. Gradually, a shift came about within the organization and it was no longer just about tough adventurous stories from the past, it was about actual knowledge and skill. If you wanted to earn some extra wages, then you would dive into the water to bring your competences up to par and to actually practice. This cultural change would never have come about, if it hadn't been for Rekers, and certainly not as quickly.

THE CARRIAGE SEATS
Cultural change in an organization takes time. Collectively changing the values of adults, in a direction they do not wish to go, is usually considered impossible.[23] However, sometimes the risks of the current culture in an organization are too high and measures must be taken. Hard measures. After all, desperate times call for desperate measures. Perhaps not entirely like a 'bull in a china shop', but depending on the nature and type of the organization, you may need to set some ambitious objectives here. Within the diving community, the change was implemented immediately. Unethical behavior was addressed firmly. Rewards would be granted based on performance only. Soon, the younger generation, who understood this, began to rise. It is up to the leader to motivate and stimulate them and to show them the trust that they deserve. The leader will have to communicate his concerns to his people and instill in them the urgent need for change. This requires a vulnerable attitude. Subsequently, he must create support for the rest of the management

---

[23] G. Hofstede, G.J. Hofstede – *Allemaal andersdenkenden*; about cultural differences; Business Contact, Amsterdam 2005

team and reward any successes.[24]

The leader creates a team around him, people with the same objectives that he has. The entire team knows which way you want to go and everybody wants to put in their best effort. The team makes the policy, follows the policy and promotes the policy.

Building blocks of leadership:
Decisive, tough, ambition

---

[24] J. Kotter, H. Rathgeber – Onze ijsberg smelt - succesvol veranderen in moeilijke omstandigheden; about successful changes under difficult circumstances Business Contact, Amsterdam, Antwerp, 2008

6. IN AFGHANISTAN

People who listen a lot and listen open-mindedly, are often those who have most to tell
-Godfried Bomans- (1913 – 1971)

The circumstances under which you lead may differ significantly. Thus could include different locations in various countries, many nationalities with a different cultural background, or a country where there is a conflict situation. In this chapter, we will address leadership in an international environment where cultural differences demand extra attention. If this is happening in a country engulfed in a conflict situation that makes it all the more interesting.

WHO GOES?
'I'll just get right to it,' Rekers said, *'I have a letter here from the Commander of the Armed Forces, stating that the Defense Diving Group – that's us –'* he continued, as he looked up from the letter *'as of November 20, is to provide a diving officer as Counter IED expert for the southern provinces in Afghanistan. Gentlemen, this is four weeks from now,'* he nonchalantly continued, *'and this is for a period of six months.'*

I needed this to sink in for a minute. Did he actually say 'diving officer of the Defense Diving Group? In four weeks? Counter IED - Countering Improvised Explosive Devices? Isn't that the same thing that what we refer to as roadside bombs? I looked at the people around the large table and realized what the consequences might be for me. Since the reorganization was in an evaluation phase, the highest levels of management would not sacrifice themselves. One colleague was going to be transferred and one other had only recently returned from Afghanistan. That left just André and me. I pictured myself at André's wedding just a few weeks ago, so in my mind I crossed out that option. I looked up at the rest of the people around me and knew that all of this essentially meant 'Good luck in Afghanistan, Jochen.'

At that moment, Rekers started to talk again. *'I expect you to send me an e-mail before Friday, stating why you might object, or maybe think that you cannot go. Decision on Monday.'*

I had to think about this. Did he say before Friday, end-of-day? But today is my last day before my weekend starts, I thought. For the past year-and-a-half, I had been in school in Amsterdam, every Friday, studying 'Operational Auditing'. This post-doctorate study cost me a lot of time and money. While I was thinking about this, somebody else proposed to send this mail no later than Monday morning. This gave me some more room to work.

The mission was a trainer's job out of the NATO Headquarters in Kandahar. It was from here that operations for the southern provinces of Afghanistan were directed. The training officer was responsible for training ISAF troops in how to detect and counter roadside bombs. How this was to take shape, was not very clear. The job was vacant at present, but one thing was clear, it would mean a lot of travelling across the southern provinces. It would also require gathering a lot of knowledge about these so-called roadside bombs, about finding them and the conceptual, strategic plan to counter them. Even as I walked back to my office, I was already contemplating the consequences that this possible deployment might mean for me. Afghanistan, for heaven's sake, what business did I have going there?

At night, when I was at home, I asked myself what I really thought of the situation. I realized that it would be a challenge. If I were looking back on my life fifty years down the line, I would want it to have been an interesting ride. That was one of the main reasons I had sought out job at the Defense Department. I weighed everything a bit more and concluded that, in an ideal situation, I could end up with a great deployment in the bag, while staying on track with my education.

I went into my study and sat down behind my desk, still unable to come to terms with it. I turned on my laptop and started writing an e-mail. Where to begin, what would be my angle? Do I really want to go? Or is it something I absolutely want to avoid? I wondered what the chances were that I would be going. If I were the commander of my unit, who would I send? This question made it all clear for me. I had better write an e-mail confirming my availability, where I explicitly weighed both the interests of the organization and my own interests. I was done in a couple of minutes. I read what I had written on the screen in front of me: *With reference to the assignment to provide a diving officer for a position in Afghanistan, please consider the following:*

We work in an organization where deployment is part of the job. I believe nobody should think otherwise. However, I do find it important that both the interests of the organization as well the interests of the individual should be considered. Appointing someone and ordering that person to go will only serve to solve the short-term problems. In my opinion, it would be better to allow everyone to have a say in the decision. I also believe that operations should be affected by this as little as possible.

Considering the current political developments, the shortage of staff on the Explosive Ordnance Disposal unit and the possibility of not incurring a delay in my studies, I would like to voice my preference to be the first to fill this vacancy.

In specific terms: Yes, I am prepared to fill the first vacancy in Afghanistan, provided that:

I will be able to complete my classes and exams for the current period at the University of Amsterdam;

I will be given the opportunity to use study facilities on location and be able to return to the Netherlands in time to attend the next round of regular exams;

The objectives and operating procedures of my department will be continued.

Please contact me, should there be any specific questions regarding the above.

With kind regards,

I turned off the computer and decided to send this e-mail message on Monday morning.

PROACTIVE

Of course, I could have stuck my head in the sand when I heard '*Gentlemen, we from diving operations have to provide an EOD officer in Afghanistan in four weeks.*' Just keep your head down there, don't move around too much and hope you don't get picked, but I decided to take the initiative and make the best of it. Obviously, you need to know how and when to pick your battles and you shouldn't want to stand at the forefront of everything, but you often have perfect sense when such a moment arrives. This was one of those moments. There was a good chance that I would be appointed. The interests of the organization were just too high. By presenting myself as a 'volunteer', I would at least have some influence and I could, in any case, point out my conditions. Besides this, I would also be building some credit, which might serve me well later. I also considered the job as a training officer as a useful contribution to the mission. We had seen too much devastation from those roadside bombs. How better to contribute to this mission than by training people to prevent these types of attacks? Finally, I also saw it as personal enrichment to take on this international individual deployment.

In times when what is expected of you seems insurmountable, it is best to take the initiative yourself. Don't hope it will all go away, but show your best side and direct the preconditions in such a way that they cater to your wishes. Make it a win-win situation. Any manager and leader will appreciate this proactive, flexible and solution-oriented attitude in his people, as will his people appreciate it in him.

> **Building blocks of leadership:**
> *Proactive, flexible, solution-oriented*

MILITARY TOUR LEADER

Quite soon after sending my e-mail, I received a reaction from Rekers. Apparently, my e-mail message had been well-received and he praised my positive attitude. A couple of hours later, I got the highly anticipated answer.

'We will first fly to Minad,' the friendly stewardess on the airplane told me. 'Minad, Minad,' I thought as I flew across the map of the world in my mind, but it didn't ring a bell. Six hours later, in the early morning, as I stood waiting next to the runway of the deserted airport near Dubai, I knew it. Minad, a military airport, for flights to Afghanistan only. Everywhere I looked, there was sand, except for the odd ugly military barracks placed there 'temporarily.'

An army warrant officer yelled *'If you hear your name, follow me to the luggage area where you will find your gear. You will get your flak jackets and your helmets out and the rest of your stuff, you will place on the right pallet. Place the jacket and helmet in military order of departure at the back of that building.'* He pointed to a building across the street. *'You may take only one piece of luggage with you. I repeat, one piece. One laptop constitutes one piece. Everything else goes on the pallet.'*

From the corner of my eye, I saw two people in civilian attire, a petite and pretty lady with long black hair and a skinny Dutchman who looked familiar. The two didn't get much attention from the group of soldiers. By this time, the sun in Minad was starting to make its presence felt. The temperature hit at least 30 degrees Celsius and what little shelter there was, was occupied by smoking service members. Then I noticed the civilian fumbling with two flak jackets and two helmets. A jacket like that weighs at least 33 pounds. You don't just hang that from your arm. As expected, he dropped everything within seconds. Since nobody made a move to help him and I was curious to find out who they were, I stood up to give him a hand. Thus began a day full of good conversations.

FROM THE EIGHT O'CLOCK NEWS

'Do tell?' I asked with enthusiasm. *'What are two civilians doing, coming to Afghanistan by military aircraft?'* He looked at me as if to say 'finally someone who wants to talk to a couple of clumsy civilians' then he told me that they were working on a report in connection with the death of private Timo. Timo had been stationed in Uruzgan and had died a summer ago, after an attack by the Taliban. *'Coincidentally, I know Timo's parents very well. In order to come to terms with the death of their son, they wanted to get in contact with the surviving relatives of the six Afghan children who died in the same bomb attack. Unfortunately, it was impossible to realize this.'* He paused for a moment, kicked at a small stone and continued. *'Then I got the idea to make a report*

111

about how Timo's parents in the Netherlands coped with the loss of their son and share this with the parents of the children who lost their lives at the same time. In short, I already filmed a part in the Netherlands about Timo and how he approached life. I am now going to show this film to the surviving relatives in Afghanistan. I think it would be quite overwhelming to also display the sorrow of the people there and tell the stories of the children who died. This way, both sides of the story are highlighted.' The sincerity of the man and his mission deeply impressed me. When I got back to the group, I heard my name being called to find my stuff for the next flight. Shortly after, I got on a bus that took me to an air-conditioned waiting room. They told me that I was on the second shift. I was going to fly to Kandahar, by way of Tarin Kowt. I would just have to wait for seven hours. While I was checking out the waiting room, a room about the size of a small gym with a pool table and one large television from which music was blaring with about twenty camp beds, I saw the two civilians sitting at a small table. This time, I decided to introduce myself properly and join them at their table.

The man was Gijs, a well-known journalist. The lady was Tabida, his camerawoman and also a journalist. Gijs had approached her specifically for this assignment because he anticipated that it might pose a problem for him to interview mothers and other female family members. The Afghan culture, especially the relationship between men and women, is significantly different than it is in Western cultures. The hours fled by once I sat down at their table. Gijs had travelled the world for over ten years. Wherever there was trouble, Gijs would be there to report the news. His work had made him famous and he was in high demand. After the death of four Dutch reporters in El Salvador, he noticed that he had become increasingly fearful and that he was no longer able to do his job the way he felt he should. He decided to go work as an editor in radio for a couple of years, after which he ended up in television. He said, 'I guess I have this thing for live images.' This is how he got into the news, getting his kicks from the excitement around live broadcasts. But after years of this work, having reported on events like the Gulf War, an airplane crashing into an Amsterdam apartment building, a fireworks disaster in Enschede and the events of 9/11, horrible things had become too much for Gijs and he called it a day. He told some wonderful stories in a very entertaining manner. I clung to his every word.

CURIOUS

Talking to people and showing a genuine interest can be very enriching. I found it incomprehensible that in an airplane filled with soldiers and just two civilians, nobody had even exchanged a single word with them. I was curious. I also felt a bit sorry for Gijs, with his clumsiness in the Minad heat, but I was particularly interested in the reasons why they would hop a military flight to Afghanistan. Looking back at this, I was glad I had offered them my help. I got to know a whole new world. Everything for that one news item. You can learn a lot from other people; you can share experiences with them and thus expand your own frame of reference. Of course, we study, we read books and we watch current affairs shows to gather knowledge, to remain up-to-date and to be able to engage in conversations, however, quite often, that knowledge is just out there for the taking, in wonderful, educational, moving stories. A leader must be inquisitive by nature. He wants to know why certain matters are different, or why they are the way they are. This natural curiosity ensures that you ask questions, that you start talking to people. Curiosity and drive to find the answers is a characteristic that is inextricably connected to leadership.

A leader not only displays curiosity outside, but also within the organization. After all, being inquisitive ensures that you show sincere interest in your staff. It is but a small effort to walk through the organization and feed this curiosity, but it generates such great success. The people feel that they are being heard and they see the leader as empathetic, sincere and curious.

> **Building blocks of leadership:**
> *Interested, curious*

TO KANDAHAR

After hours of waiting in a hall that was simply too cold and too white and where the outside temperature was too high, we finally received word that we were being picked up by a British C130, an aircraft used by the British military to move their troops to Afghanistan.

In the distance, I could hear the sound of the engines approaching. Within minutes, the sound swelled to a deafening roar, but I still could not detect where it was coming from. It had gone pitch dark in no time. It was as if someone had pulled the sun down by a rope.

Suddenly, I saw an airplane moving forward on the runway. Fortunately, the propellers stopped turning and the incredible noise ebbed away. The plane fueled up first and then we were asked to get in a straight line for boarding. Not the way that you would expect on a commercial airline with friendly smiles from the flight attendant, mind you. This was a rear hatch that was lowered and an English NCO, the loadmaster, asking us in a friendly but urgent voice to get on board and sit down on the benches that were lined up along the length of the aircraft.

Arrival in Afghanistan in a C130

The benches were very uncomfortable, more like steel frames with nets attached to them. Eventually, we were packed in there like sardines. *'Guys, quick briefing'* the loadmaster shouted over the noisy propellers that had just started up again. *'These are emergency exits.'* he said pointing left and right. *'If you want to use them, you're already in deep shit. For the last bit of this trip, I'll ask you to take seats and wear helmets and armor. The flight will take three and a half hours. Let's get Rollin'.* 'Did he just say three and a half hours?' I thought to myself. 'Folded up like that? I was never going to make it!'

Meanwhile, the airplane started rolling and the roar became so bad that I had to look for my earplugs. We were up in the air within moments and I could feel my stomach churning with all the antics pulled by the pilot. A rollercoaster ride paled in comparison. However, soon after we had taken off, it was signaled that we didn't have to stay in our seats. The question was, 'Where would we go?' After we had boarded, they rolled two huge pallets in behind us filled with duffle bags, taking up any free space that was left. I was so uncomfortable in that seat though that I quickly got up and stood on top of it. I'd had enough of standing like that after a few minutes, so I leaned against one of the pallets and stared straight ahead, as if in a daze. It had gotten cold now too and my legs were starting to stiffen up. Noise, stiff legs and a clock that was ticking far too slow made me start to miss that cold white hall and the heat in Minad. That was quite the paradise compared to this. After hanging around like that for about two hours, shifting my weight from one leg to the other, we got the signal to get dressed in full gear and take our seats in the hammocks again. *'Take your seats, we'll soon arrive in Kandahar,'* the loadmaster shouted. I thought we'd made good time, but as it turned out, we hadn't made a stop in Uruzgan but instead went straight to Kandahar. The lights on the aircraft went out, a window was partially opened, probably to drop the already cold temperature on the aircraft even more, and I was ready for landing. After about an hour of sitting there, ready for landing, I realized the relativity of the words 'We'll soon arrive' and also that it was probably policy for us to fly over Afghanistan in full gear. One thing more was very clear to me: this was no pleasure ride to some sunny holiday destination. Far from it.

THE C-IED BRANCH
'Hey, Tjo-han,' I heard in a Canadian accent. In front of me was a big, broad Canadian with an even bigger smile. I had arrived at my place of work on the base in Kandahar. After a short night of restless sleep, I was finally here. *Welcome, you have arrived,'* said Mike. The rest of the club also got up to introduce themselves. I heard all sorts of names and *'Sir'* this and *'Sir'* that. The one that stood out the most, however, proved to be the leader of this club, Colonel Tim. He was a short, broad-shouldered American Army Ranger, no taller than 5'5". He shouted his greeting. I learned later that this was his way of communicating.

I shook many hands and got a lot of information right away. The biggest challenge was all of the different English dialects: British, Scottish, American, Canadian, Australian, Nepalese-English, Indian-English and that's not including all of the local dialects from each of those

115

places. I would never be able to concentrate and listen to this all day. It drained all of my energy. And to think that I had to memorize all the information I was given, the names, the main action points. It was a difficult task, in any case, especially because I had not slept properly for days. Fortunately, I found comfort in the fact that things were not as bad as they had initially seemed. Things that were really important would certainly be repeated. Besides, there would probably be people who had more difficulty with English than I did.

Mike was also a diving officer. Imagine that, two navy divers in the Afghan desert. Not only was he trained as a diver, my Canadian friend was also a trained commando who had learned quite a few tricks. His unit in Canada jumped out of airplanes in diving gear just to crawl into a submarine that was lying in wait. They spent as much time in forests as they did at, on or in the water. That was quite different than my job as Head of the Diving Technical Research Center. I willingly let myself be swept along by Mike's enthusiasm, every now and then ignoring the 'fuck this' and 'fuck that' from my 'little' American big boss.

LUCKY
After a trip of a couple of days to the province of Uruzgan, I had returned to the base in Kandahar, which felt a bit like home now. Just getting back to the old routine – going through my e-mail after breakfast, then working out with Mike and finishing with a cup of coffee at Tim Hortens'. The Canadian coffee proprietor was earning big bucks at headquarters. I actually enjoyed this morning routine.

After lunch, I got up from my desk and was walking towards the latrines, when I heard a bang in the distance. I thought they were clearing old mines somewhere near the airfield, which was not unusual war time, but a fraction later, I heard and felt a rocket whiz past my head. It felt as if a tennis ball had been hit right past my ear, but I felt it in my bones. My heart skipped a number of beats and I braced for the impact, but none came. For a second, I was rooted to the spot, perplexed. I had lost the urge to go to the bathroom when I realized that a 107mm rocket had just flown past my head. I contemplated what I would do and decided to just let it be. My heart rate dropped to normal again, as if nothing had happened. I walked back to the barracks and told the men '*I guess the air alarm will be sounding soon.*' My colleagues looked up at me questioningly and indeed, at just that moment, the alarm went off.

116

We closed the door, and I had heard one make impact. I had almost head-butted one rocket already, so running for cover would be too little, too late now. Instead of sitting in a bunker for an hour, waiting for the 'all clear' sign, we decided to just get on with the job at hand. I thought about that rocket. What if I'd had a really bad day and all the bad luck would've piled up into one heap? I wondered if the 'gentlemen of the Taliban' would not prefer to sit at home with their families, rather than firing off random lucky shots at a NATO camp. On the other hand, this happened multiple times a week and I unconsciously became immune to it. After I got back to the Netherlands, I heard that a rocket had hit close to the queue in front of Tim Hortens'. I wondered how often I had stood in that spot.

BLACK SUNDAY

Hans was the second Dutchman at the C-IED club. He was about fifty years old and felt a bit out of place in this strange environment. His biggest problem was his understanding of English, but his enthusiasm and the fact that he tried to hide his limited confidence, worked in his favor. Hans had no knowledge of explosives or IEDs. He was a liaison officer and never, in his thirty years of loyal service to the Army, had he been deployed. Everything was new and exciting and certainly outside of his comfort zone. 'Let's just hope it all works out,' I remember thinking.

Hans was immediately thrown into the lion's den a few days later. A Canadian vehicle hit a roadside bomb. The first information we received mentioned three injured soldiers. An hour later, it turned out that at least one Canadian had died and four others were wounded. Mike was back in Canada on holiday, so the initial report was received by Hans. He had no idea what to do. First, one of the Canadians had tried to phone him from the Canadian headquarters, but Hans blamed the poor connection for not being able to understand him. In the end, the call took fifteen minutes, but nothing came of it. According to procedure, we were supposed to be at the helicopter within thirty minutes to collect evidence at the scene. Organizing this in Mike's absence was Hans' responsibility. None of it sunk in with Hans and because of the rising stress level, he forgot to carry out the simplest of tasks, like informing the boss or putting a team together to go investigate.

Hans really had no idea what he was doing. What was worse, he had no clue how to get control of the situation. It was obvious that he was the wrong man in the wrong place. He had no knowledge and experience to fall back on, just bits and pieces of information in his head and no clear final objective to work towards. This was a black Sunday for Hans and for the Canadian armed forces. The next day was dedicated to the farewell ceremony for the Canadian soldier. Sadly, we had many such ceremonies at the Kandahar headquarters.

TAKING RESPONSIBILITY

Unfortunately, Hans had to learn the hard way how to get a grip on such extraordinary situations. He wasn't to blame, however. As his chief in the C-IED Branch, Mike really should've prepared Hans better, before he went on leave. Also the 'little' big boss should've been clear about who would direct operations in Mike's absence. Hans had no knowledge and experience and his communication skills were way below par. As soon as things became stressful, it all turned into one narrow tunnel in his head, while the clock was ticking. The American boss should've taken responsibility and directed operations himself in Mike's absence. Or maybe he should've appointed someone else, someone who did have the knowledge and experience.

However, the boss hid behind the fact that he did not have the time to take on the job himself, so he left Hans hanging out to dry. Murphy's Law struck when Hans was immediately charged with dealing with the attack. Regretfully, this was not a drill, but a real attack where people's lives were at stake. Both the boss and Mike could have and should have prepared Hans better for his task. Even a simple list of things to do could've made a difference. Hans, on the other hand, also should not have settled for such poor preparation himself. He should've proactively asked for clear guidelines about how to do his job. Within the Defense Department, we had a slogan - 7 Ps - and this was not for nothing: Proper Planning and Preparation Prevents a Piss Poor Performance. In short, if you prepare well, you will prevent poor execution.

> **Building blocks of leadership:**
> *Proactive, responsible*

THE REASON FOR OUR STAY

I had just returned from another trip through the southern provinces of Afghanistan, when Steve invited me to join him for dinner. Steve was the second man of the C-IED branch. This English EOD major had a lot of knowledge about things, but he was always too modest to elaborate on this. We got to know each other better and better over dinner. I told him all about my diving, my assessment, the assignments, sports diving and diving accidents we handled in our diving tank in Den Helder. By that time, the conversation had taken an entirely different course as we talked about people dying while diving and some extraordinary accidents I had witnessed in the past years.

Steve then started to tell me about one of his less enjoyable jobs. In 1995, when he was a young officer deployed to Bosnia, he became an officer of the pioneers. As an additional task, he was the leader of a unit responsible for the mass graves in the region. What he had seen there was unimaginable. '*You won't believe what it's like when you have to fish fifty people out of a water well,*' Steve said. '*Then to try to collect all the limbs and to tag as many items that might be linked to a person. Subsequently, I had to go and ask the local population if they could please help out and see if they saw anything they recognized,*' Steve continued. '*So if anyone did indeed recognize something, then it was up to us to ask for a name, a place of residence and that type of information, so you could link all of this to the remains.*' I fell silent, hearing Steve's story, and I listened to him in horror, but also in amazement. Amazed by his calm composure.

'*You don't want to know the things I've seen. You won't believe what people can do to others. If people are just dead, so be it, but mutilated children, pregnant women, terribly, horribly abused, so bad, you would not want to go through that, Jochen.*' Steve was visibly shaken up by his own story. I asked him if his people didn't have any problem with all this and how he dealt with it in his role as a leader. He said that he did this with a team of thirty men and some of them really struggled to cope with it. '*At night, they would drink lots and lots of beer behind closed doors, with nobody else around. They would talk about it a lot. Together, talking, talking and more talking. That helped.*'

I thought about this -the year 1995. At that time, I was still in secondary school, living with my parents. That was the year that I was giving my secondary school teachers hell. What a difference.

119

LISTENING IS AN ART

Why did Steve start to tell me about the tough times he'd had in Bosnia? You don't just recollect painful memories, for the sake of a good story. Something happens in a conversation between two people, making it possible to talk sincerely, openly and trustingly. This happens for two reasons. First, there is the recipient's ability to empathize, instinctively understanding the other person. How does the other person feel? What does he want to share? What doesn't he want to share? More important is the second reason, which is the art of listening. Really listening. Asking the right questions, or sometimes allowing for a moment of silence, when silence is desired. Listening without providing solutions. Listening without reshaping the information from your own frame of reference.

We are inclined to listen and fixate on problems. The real art lies in listening and focusing on the exceptions, positive messages and auxiliary resources, without providing feedback.[25] Listening also means analyzing the message and interacting, proving that you are actually listening. This way, you show that you understand, but also that you are interested. Listening properly should be part of a leader's toolkit as this is indispensable for all leaders. It is unavoidable that, as a leader, you will be involved in difficult conversations, perhaps with an employee who has lost a loved one, or who is involved in a divorce, or maybe just needs to get something of his/her chest while going through a hard time. How you deal with this is a question of sensitivity, experience, tact and patience. You have to give people room to tell their story.

> **Building blocks of leadership:**
> *Empathy, listening skills, tact*

---

[25] L. Cauffman – *Simpel werkt het best; Oplossingsgericht management & coaching;* about solution-directed management and coaching; Lemma Utrecht, 2005

MOTHER DUCK

It was during the absence of the Branch Chief when I noticed that we were all running after the mother duck like little ducklings. It made me think of my worst experiences with the commander on the navy frigate, a couple of years earlier. Here, all the 'unit heads' ran after the commander like young ducks. '*EYYYYYY*', he would shout from behind his desk, '*What time are we going to eat?*' Most of the time, he would ask this when he noticed that Hans and I were getting ready to go. We would then give him a time and we knew from experience that it would take at least thirty minutes more before we would actually walk out of the Branch. I wasn't bothered by this in the first few weeks. Adapting was the creed. Now that the Chief had been away for a couple of weeks, I noticed that it started to annoy me more and more. This afternoon, Hans and I had been waiting for twenty minutes already, but the Mother Duck still showed no signs that he intended to go. '*We're off to lunch,*' we yelled and decided to go without him.

We must've been eating lunch for about ten minutes when the rest walked past us and sat down at a table near us. The chief looked at me, shrugging his shoulders as if to say 'Where were you guys?' I responded with a gesture as if to say 'What am I, nuts?' but I maintained a friendly smile. I decided that in the future, I would just adapt or clearly let him know that we would be eating earlier. It's not like he was a bad guy or anything…

DIPLOMACY

Working in a multinational environment also means dealing with different cultures - other opinions, other ways of working, other relations and responsibilities. Suddenly you begin questioning your frame of reference – it may not be the right one anymore. In an environment where different cultures come together, you will need to assume a more reserved approach and realize that your way of working and handling situations may be strange to others. Diplomacy is often defined as 'the management of international relations by negotiation.'[26] So, the diplomat is a master in managing, negotiating and maintaining international relations.

In some military cultures, the boss will holler when it's time to go and eat. This is the signal to say 'People, we will go eat when I am ready

---

[26] J. Melissen – *Diplomatie; Radarwerk van de internationale politiek* – about diplomacy as an instrument of international politics; Van Gorcum, Assen, 1999

to go eat.' The Dutchman will then think, 'I will go eat whenever I want to and I have no intention of waiting for you.' That typical Dutch reaction is 'leveling' and often corrective behavior, the figurative finger wagging to make it clear to people that they are not doing things right. But you have to be able to adapt to other cultures somehow. Our desire to go eat alone was not right. This may well be just a small example, but it illustrates how some things are looked at differently. The Chief had no idea, after all. To him, it is the most normal thing in the world that people should wait for him. Some cultures love to create teams and as a team, you present yourself to the outside world. So what can be better than walking to the mess hall like a mother duck, with the little ducklings on your tail? It is not up to you to lecture the Chief at such a time, you should adapt to the different customs. Perhaps you may find a more diplomatic way to make it clear that you or others prefer to use a different method.

> **Building blocks of leadership:**
> *Empathy, listening skills, tact*

ULTRA CREPIDARIAN

'Stress is like an armored suit, Jochen,' Steve suddenly called out to me. He was standing in the doorway of the porch, smoking a cigar. It made me laugh and I recalled our conversation about stress from a few weeks ago. What is stress and how do you deal with it? As an EOD officer, Steve also saw his fair share of action in Belfast, with IRA attacks. Steve's way of dealing with stress was rather simple. Face it and fight it. A typical rugby theory, which I quite liked. Stress was like a harness to Steve. He would put it on and enter the battlefield. *'Stress is like an armored suit. Just strap it on and get into it!'*

He turned around and blew some cigar smoke into the branch and he asked, *'Jochen, do you know what Ultra Crepidarian means'*? I thought about this, but had absolutely no idea what he was talking about. He seemed as if he was trying to suppress his laughter and he wasn't very successful at it. He came inside and showed me his notebook where he had written on the inner sleeve:

'Ultra Crepidarian: people who comment on matters beyond their limits or understanding.'

I read it at least three times and I thought it was a brilliant sentence. 'Ultra Crepidarian.' I should remember that one. However, the more I thought about it, the less meaningful it became. Doesn't everybody walk into that trap? On the other hand, we also had this saying, 'In the land of the blind, the one-eyed man is king.' But Steve came up with a practical example. *'Let's say you're in a meeting and somebody else knows everything better and talks a lot of nonsense all the time - then you're dealing with an Ultra Crepidarian. It's not like you need to keep your mouth shut all the time, but ask yourself whether or not you are the person to make the call on that subject at that time.'* I thought this was an excellent translation of the 'Ultra Crepidarian.' I decided to write this down in my notebook as well.

STRESS

Everybody experiences stress in a different way. Everybody has different moments of stress. What's important is how you handle it. As soon as you are in a stressful situation, the brain starts working. The sympathetic nervous system will produce a fight or flight response. Your breathing will quicken, your heart will start pounding and your field of vision will be reduced. Then a second system will start working. The pituitary gland in your brain orders the production of cortisol, which will raise your blood sugar level and your metabolism will kick in. Unfortunately, the stress system doesn't only react to physical threats, but because of our awareness, also to mental threats.

Research has shown that extreme or chronic stress during the first four years of a person's life will make that person more vulnerable to later stressors. On the other hand, stressful experiences that are not too over-whelming will make children more defensible.[27] In short, stress has a purpose and it may work in a positive manner, as long as it occurs in mild doses.

---

[27] R. de Jongh; *Wat stress doet met je brein(Wat doet stress met ons lichaam en brein?* – article about what stress does to your body and brain – Psychologie magazine, May 2010

The effects of stress on the body and the brain depend on how we deal with it: our coping strategy. There are two variants of this. First, there is problem focused or active coping, where we immediately address the problem. Those who approach a problem very actively will show less stress in both the sympathetic nervous system and in cortisol production. Then there is defensive or emotion-focused coping. Here we avoid the problem and we attempt to influence our emotions. Defensive coping leads to greater and more prolonged stress. It can be useful, if you can manage to keep the stress out completely.

It's clear that a leader will need to control his stress level very well. Steve had found a clear way to handle stress for himself. He clearly applied active coping by viewing stress as an armored vest. Instead of walking away from a situation, he would meet it head on and fight it. His imaginary vest gave him the sense that he could master the situation, a feeling as if he were invincible. Other people will seek peace. They will sit down to get their breathing under control, think of a peaceful moment and then step back into their environment. Everybody has his own way of dealing with stress. Stress, in any case, ensures that your image of the truth is limited, while what a leader needs is just the opposite: a clear overall view. He must be able to separate main issues and side issues and make sure he does not get sucked in by the details of the moment. So, stress is a poor counselor for the leader.

The following steps will help you to deal with stress and increase your internal room to maneuver:

1. Acknowledge when you experience stress at the right time. **Recognize** the signals and symptoms

2. Ensure that you set the right **priorities** in the environment that causes you stress.

3. Take a step back. Do not allow yourself to get sucked into the problem, but maintain an **overview**.

4. Think of solutions, think 'out-of-the-box' and ask yourself '**What should I do now**'?

5. Widen the internal room to maneuver by using **the knowledge of others**.

6. Emanate **calm and confidence.**

7. Take a **decision** and apply active coping. Every decision is better than no decision and you can work from there.

If you follow these steps, stress does not need to have a negative effect on your leadership qualities.

> **Building blocks of leadership:**
> *Stress-resistant, self-knowledge,*
> *decisiveness*

SNAPPED

As always, Sundays were quiet days at headquarters. Everybody started working a bit later than normal, most of the time this was around 10 o'clock. I came in at 9:45am and I saw that it was fairly busy already. Hans was behind his desk and some workers were putting the finishing touches on a new floor, so things were pretty busy. '*Good morning, Hans.*' He looked up and I could tell his eyes were watery. Something in Hans must have snapped. *Come on, let's step outside for a minute,*' I said right away.

Hans hadn't slept all night. Problems at home had kept him awake. Then he had come to work and found a full mailbox. The boss came in with a question that he didn't understand right away. It all became too much for him, like a perfectionist in a working environment that he only half understood. The combination of his first tour, his frustrations over the English language, his frustrations over the loudmouth American, his bad night, problems at home and something had snapped. It is strange to watch the emotions of a 51-year-old captain get the better of him and make him cry. Hans wanted nothing more than to get on the first plane out and fly home but after long talks, tears and time, Hans felt a lot better…after a while.

How much productivity will you get out of an employee who would prefer nothing else but go home? Feeling homesick plays a huge part here and there's not a lot you can do about that. What you can do, however, is to ensure that the preconditions are such, that at least you are comfortable in your job. Hans was a clear example of the emotional, passive, coping strategy. Even if he'd wanted to address the problem actively, he'd still be faced with the annoying language barrier.

You are sent to a far-off country. You know you will be working in a multinational environment. You know the working language will be English, which you have not mastered very well. If you are going to work as a representative of a country or a company, you should make sure you make proper preparations. As an employer, you should ensure that you send the right people, at the very least, people who speak the working language. However, there is also the responsibility of the employee: you. Make sure that you speak the language required to carry out your work. This speaks to communication skills. As has been clearly shown in the example at headquarters in Afghanistan, if you don't speak English, you're out of the game. You will not be taken seriously anymore and it will take too much time to explain everything to you again. You have but one chance. One chance to make it count and if you have to speak, do it with flair (we use the term 'flair' on purpose: flair is a behavior – it differs from charisma in that you can teach yourself to do something, for instance present in front of an audience, in an engaging way… with flair). Make sure your presence is felt, speak in a loud and clear voice and ensure that nobody wants to or is able to overlook you. You may have the best ideas, but if you can't make them clear to others, they will stay ideas in your head and they will eventually die in silence.

> **Building blocks of leadership:**
> *Communication skills, flair*

SMALL SCARS

People must be willing to work with you as a leader. They must at all times support you and have faith in the decisions you make. They will not do this just because they think you are a nice person, someone with whom they would enjoy getting a cup of coffee. No, they should have unlimited trust in you as a leader; trust in you when the organization is doing poorly and you want to turn things around; trust in you when you lead them into battle. The leader has the ability to get the people to follow him even under difficult circumstances.

You do not create this blind trust by befriending everybody, sometimes you will need to make unpleasant, harsh decisions. Decisions that may be painful but will be in the best interests of the group or which will serve the best result. The challenge for a leader is to do this at the right moment. Sometimes you must be tough and clear, and at other times, you must be understanding and sympathetic. If a leader acts as an empathetic coach, he can make people work for him, without being everybody's friend.

Hans clearly needed to have some sort of coaching in his work. The problems he encountered with his first deployment, the lack of knowledge, the problems at home, and his poor command of the English language regularly got the better of him. At moments like this, an employee will be less productive. However, it is not like you have replacements lined up, waiting to take over his tasks in a country like Afghanistan. What it comes down to is coaching. The coach may contribute to people performing 'better' and as such, ensuring a better product or a better process.

> **Building blocks of leadership:**
> *Trustworthiness, decisiveness, tough, empathy*

When I returned, I felt very positive about what, in the end, had been four months in Afghanistan. I had learned a lot and I had seen a lot, although it was not all positive. Three weeks after I left Afghanistan, Hans had a break-down and returned home to the Netherlands with a severe hangover from his deployment. Then there were the heavy attacks that the Dutch had to endure in Uruzgan, and also all the human remains of all the other nationals that left Afghanistan by way of Kandahar. There were a lot of ceremonies and every ceremony left a deep impression. Despite all of the misery we faced in Afghanistan, the experience was enriching. It was my first real introduction into collaboration in a multinational environment.

7. CULTURAL DIFFERENCES

We all resemble each other in that we are different in every detail.
-Julien de Valckenaere- (1898 – 1958)

Working in an international environment and doing business with people of a different background has its fair share of challenges. Tolerance towards other cultures and knowledge of these cultures is essential to maintaining a good relationship. The navy had offered me the opportunity to work for NATO headquarters in Spain. During this time, I regularly encountered cultural differences. As a leader, not only should you be aware of this, but you will also be required to deal with it properly. It may simply be a case of conflicting ideas. Again, you should beware of deciding or judging too quickly, but first make sure you are well-informed about local customs and cultural differences. The time will come when you will be asked to lead in the way that you think best serves the environment. If your environment changes and you are forced to work together closely for an extended period, it will quickly become clear that leadership is not for everyone.

GARLIC DOESN'T STINK
'I'll be there at eight,' I told Pedro through the phone. Pedro was a fellow officer from Spain who was working at the headquarters as a doctor but his duties mostly consisted of overseeing medical advice and logistical planning. Pedro was a so-called "Subject Matter Expert." He had not seen patients in a long time. I found that hard to understand, a highly educated physician, a man with an MD, walking around a NATO base in a major's uniform answering questions from some general every now and then. Pedro was fine with it, however, and he and I had become buddies.

Pedro had invited me to a place called 'Las Rozas' and eight o'clock seemed like a proper time to meet. I imagined we would be going to the restaurant at nine and Pedro would have me taste the tapas that he, as a Spaniard, enjoyed. Things did not go as I had imagined, though. I arrived at Pedro's a little before eight o'clock and we had a nice conversation while enjoying a beer. By nine, I was starting to get hungry and I was already contemplating the things I had waiting for me the next day. My alarm was set for 6:30, after all. We still had to get to the restaurant, eat and then drive home, but Pedro wanted to show me all sorts of things and he didn't seem to be intent on going to dinner yet. He thought ten o'clock was the proper Spanish time for that. *'Let's use my car,'* Pedro said. *'We have to go into the city center and it'll probably be very busy.'* I thought about that for a minute. That would mean that after dinner I would also have to drive back to pick up my car and then drive home. I could see myself getting to bed very late. A few minutes later, I was sitting next to Pedro, on our way to downtown Las Rozas. Pedro drove like a real Spaniard. He wasn't horribly concerned with the other people on the road too much. 'I'm driving here, so you can get out of my way.' Parking was not much different. Bump the car in front a bit, bump the one behind you a bit and you were parked. I was a bit irritated by the anti-social parking habits, as I pictured this happening to my car, but anyway, so many countries, so many customs, I guess.

It was now after ten in the evening, and there was just one thing on my mind - food! Once again, however, I learned that I had not fully integrated into the Spanish way of life. Pedro had first planned to get a beer at the local pub, as this was also customary when dining in Spain. Eventually, we entered the restaurant, a little after eleven o'clock. I was surprised by how busy the place still was and by how many people came in after us. Entire families with children, really young children who, in the Netherlands, would be in bed by seven o'clock. This was a late-night event. I decided to share my amazement with Pedro.

'Pedro, don't you think children should be in bed at this hour, instead of still having to eat dinner?' I asked in English. Pedro just looked at me. He didn't understand. *'Why?'* he asked. *'Well, children need their sleep. Tomorrow, they have to get up early and actually it is even too late for us. We have to work in the morning,'* I said.

'Yes, but tomorrow is tomorrow, right? We live now and now we're having a nice time and we do not think about work in the morning. It's only work. Besides, here in Madrid it is much too hot to eat earlier. This is the time when it is a bit cooler and it is very pleasant to be outside and have dinner.' We just couldn't agree on questions of productivity, lack of sleep, bedtime for kids, work, and the influence of the temperature on the economy. It was obvious we were facing a cultural barrier here. The

fact that we had to work in the morning was something he simply would not consider. *'Listen, Jochen,'* Pedro continued, *'in Spain, especially in Madrid, it is the most normal thing in the world on Friday for people to be dealing with their hangover, rather than thinking about work. Especially young people. Life doesn't revolve around work; life is the moments of joy that you have to seize when they are there. Tomorrow is another day...'*

I told Pedro that when cooking, I always considered what I was preparing. For example, if I had an important appointment the next day, I would not use any garlic. This had him completely puzzled. First of all, garlic did not stink, not the next day and not the day after that and secondly, surely you're not going to base whatever you are cooking on your work schedule for the next day, are you? In short, we were on entirely different wavelengths and this was a cultural gap that just could not be bridged.

I could follow his reasoning, though. Work is obviously a means by which to earn a living, preferably a good living. You have to do it as well as possible, however, and if this means that you have to take certain things into account, then you do it. You can have your so-called 'pleasures' on Friday night or Saturday. Our differences of opinion were not only about social considerations. There were misunderstandings that types of things were work-related as well. In the Netherlands, if I were to send an e-mail, I would expect a prompt response, even if it was just confirmation of receipt or an 'out-of-office' reply. In Spain, I would send an e-mail and then drop by the office of the recipient to invite him out for a cup of coffee. During such relaxed moments, I would briefly discuss the content of the e-mail and explain that I expected a response before the end of the week. This was not an unimportant detail. This was something that must be considered in order to do a job in a different country. These are interesting international challenges.

On the night of the dinner, I didn't get home until half past one. I lay in bed with my fat belly up in the air. 'No, this was not for me, spending my weeks like that,' I thought. 'I clearly feel better at home in northern Europe.'

DIFFERENT CULTURES
Slowly, I got acquainted with the different cultures on the base. Not just the Spanish, but also the Italian, Turkish, American, Greek, Portu-

guese, French and German. What I noticed was that if you are working with so many different nationalities, you will automatically pay more attention to your own customs and culture. You will look not only at yourself, but also at your countrymen. How do they do this? Can it be done differently? Generalization was difficult to do, but certain cultural aspects did stand out within the NATO headquarters. I also heard the opinions of others about the various cultures there. In 1980, Hofstede did some groundbreaking research into the dimensions in which cultures differ from each other and how these differences express themselves in certain personality characteristics.[28] He concluded that there are four dimensions that influence this.

1 Power distance

In case of a short power distance, the fact that others are the boss doesn't go over well. People want to feel that they are at least equal and they do not want others to impose their will on them. In the case of a greater power distance, the opposite applies. People have no problem with this distance and find it the most normal thing in the world. There is respect for authority and the power distance is accepted.

2 Individualism

In an individualist society, the individual takes center stage. The 'first person' and the people close to that person are at the core. In a collective society, the group is at the center and the individual derives his identity from that group. Confronting someone on his behavior is an attack on the group and not on the individual.

3 Masculinity

A masculine society is geared to the dominant values with a firm division of tasks, often linked to gender. The feminine society is often more focused on the quality of life, with similar roles for both men and women.

---

[28] G. Hofstede, G.J. Hofstede – *Allemaal andersdenkenden*; about cultural differences; Business Contact, Amsterdam 2005

4 Avoiding insecurity

Insecurity is something we usually experience as unpleasant. We then try to master this insecurity with guidelines, rules and arrangements. In some cultures, people like it when things are slightly informal, while in others they want everything to be clearly stipulated. Such a society is often combined with a lot of bureaucracy. In a society where not many rules have been laid down, there often is more tolerance for deviant behavior, but this freedom may also lead to the abuse of and improper use of power.

Hofstede's study determined that in countries where they spoke Roman languages, like Spain and Italy, there was a greater power distance than the countries where Germanic languages were spoken, like the Netherlands, Germany and Scandinavia. In the countries of southern Europe, people were used to great power distances and had no trouble conforming to leadership. In northern Europe and Scandinavia, it is just the opposite. The power distance is kept at a minimum here. Also, in my experience, masculine society is much more dominant in the Mediterranean countries than in it is in northern Europe. In general, the roles of men and women are similar in the north, whereas in southern Europe, traditional gender roles are maintained, that is, the tradition of male leadership, even in the home.

Individualism is more consistent with the cultures of northern Europe, while in southern Europe, community is key. Finally, in the north, there are structures, guidelines and procedures for all things. This avoidance of insecurities happens less frequently in southern Europe, where it is accepted that there are very few regulations. The distinctions so clearly phrased by Hofstede, were very obvious during my experiences in Madrid and my earlier deployment to Afghanistan.

If you act as a leader abroad, you will need to be aware of the cultural differences, in order to be effective. An organization will therefore be required to prepare a leader or employee very well, or maybe even consider appointing local leaders.[29]

---

[29] J. Bersin; How do leadership strengths vary around the globe – article 1, November 2012

SINGING

My additional job at the NATO headquarters ensured that I was allowed to travel a lot. I was involved in improving the interoperability with non-NATO countries and preparing these countries for greater collaboration and even membership in some cases. Most of the time, this would consist of specific training or seminars. I would arrange officers from the fields of expertise in question within our headquarters and compose a team. With this team, I would travel to the country and provide training courses in the field of logistics, IT or the NATO planning process. A week of training meant I would leave on Monday, train from Tuesday to Thursday and be back in Madrid on Friday.

Quite a bit was 'expected' from the people who went along with me: travel to a foreign country, give a presentation for a foreign audience and spend a couple of days away from home meeting new people. To me, this sounded fantastic, so I found it unbelievable that it was so difficult to find volunteers to go with me the first time. There were very few people who were keen on a week in Montenegro, Bosnia, Morocco, Tunisia or Croatia, to name just a few of our destinations. Those who did come with me were a bit cautious. Not many of them had an assertive approach. Rarely did anyone go out and put on a sparkling show and I didn't understand why my colleagues were giving such lame presentations. For most of these training courses, you didn't even need to be a subject matter expert and all those poor performances reminded me of my time at the student rugby club in Eindhoven.

The rugby team practiced twice a week and just as it is on any student team, it was not only about sports. We were required to show some social skills as well. Fortunately, after years playing rugby at the Royal Naval Academy, I had developed a pretty good game. In any case, I was good enough to play for a student team in the Dutch second division. What I had not considered, were the additional qualities that were expected of a rugby-playing student. In order of importance these were: to drink beer, sing, boast and party. And so, after my first game on the student team, I found myself with an enormous jug of beer in my hand, celebrating our first win of the season. After a while, our captain started to sing a song, but not just any song. Every line he sang was a little more obscene than the one before. And everybody, except me, was singing along at the top of their lungs. After this 20-verse song, somebody else started in on the next song. Every now and then, I would recognize bits and pieces from a cadence song we had used on Texel a few years before. What struck me was that I knew six verses of this, while they were now singing about forty-four different ones. The rules were soon clear to me. The person who started the song, was supposed to finish it. This meant that nobody else knew the lyrics as well as he did or could sing as many verses as he could. If that were to happen, you end drunk very quickly, because being outdone on the song that you had started meant that you would end up on a table with an enormous pitcher of beer. This ritual would repeat itself if you started a song that had already been sung that evening, or if you disrespected the singer(s) by not listening and continuing your conversation. There were plenty of rules and you would soon master them or be forced to drink until you learned. For me this was like 'learning on the job'.

After playing for a couple of weeks, I was allowed to attend a general membership meeting of the rugby club. In good spirits, I sought out a jacket and a tie from my wardrobe. I expected some kind of formal setting where the gentlemen rugby players would demonstrate their ability to lead an association. In fact, I expected something like the board membership meetings at the Royal Naval Academy. My image of a general membership meeting turned out to be rather unrealistic.

The board was seated behind a beautiful oak table in the backroom of some pub in the inner city of Eindhoven. At first glance, the gentlemen looked crisp and clean. They all wore the same club tie, dark pants and neat shoes. However, if you looked more closely, the shoes looked well worn out and the traces of last night's beer were still evident on their clothes. Nevertheless, it looked better than a torn up rugby shirt full of holes. *'Welcome to this twelfth General Membership Meeting of the Student Rugby Club. Before we begin our meeting, I would like to propose a toast to ...'* and then they were toasting something that was total gibberish for me. I emptied my glass, and immediately hoped that this would not be repeated too often this evening. A hopeless thought. Immediately after I had finished my beer, the glass was filled again, out of one of many jugs being handed around in the meeting room. The number of members present at this meeting had now risen to about fifty, many of whom I had never seen before, although they all appeared to be former players or injured players from one of the teams.

I was particularly interested in the subjects to be discussed in this meeting, but that would have to wait because another toast was coming. Eventually, even before the agenda was addressed, the meeting was paused for a bathroom break, because the beers were starting to make their presence felt in the bladders of the board. About ten minutes and a couple of pints later, the meeting continued. I had received an agenda with twelve items on it and not one of them had been discussed yet. Finally, the first item was discussed and just before the chairman proceeded to the second one, our biggest and most competent player decided to start a song. He stood up, squeezed his eyes almost shut and turned his head upwards to the ceiling. He started singing at the top of his lungs and before I knew it, everybody had joined in. It sounded magnificent and it turned out to be a rugby version of 'Sloop John B'. I was very impressed with the song and the singing voices in our club, but that wasn't the end of it. Immediately after this, another rugby player started the next song. I noticed that the members of the board were looking a bit awkward. After all, the rules were clear: a song that was being sung could not be interrupted. It was one of the rules from the 'ten singing commandments' and eventually this was the end of the general membership meeting.

Over four hours of singing and drinking, without a single song being repeated. Obviously, the more time that went by, the smaller the repertoire there was remaining. When someone's name was called, everyone would hold their breath, waiting to see what they would come up with. Usually, this would take about two seconds and then everybody would join in. Suddenly, my name was called. I had to sing a song. Not singing was not an option, because then I would be forced to stand on a table with half a liter of beer. Besides, it had been my own choice to attend this General Membership Meeting, or even, to become a member of this student rugby club. We had learned more than just sports and how to carry a chain around during my time on Texel, so I thought it'd be smart to start a cadence song. A real navy cadence song would be just the thing, I thought. Soon everyone was singing along at the top of their lungs, waiting at the beginning of each new verse to hear me sing the first words. It went well for about five verses, maybe half of a sixth, but then I decided not to start on a seventh. That proved to be a big mistake. The gentlemen of the student rugby club knew three times as many verses to that particular song! And that was the first time that night that I found myself standing on a table going bottoms up with half a liter of beer.

Unfortunately, I had to go through that a few more times. I was about to drown in beer when I heard my name again. Something told me to go for the safest option: the Dutch national anthem, the *Wilhelmus*. Yes, I knew the first and middle verse by heart. I hadn't stood beside my bed for so many hours in the dorm at the naval academy memorizing the *Wilhelmus* and the naval cadet's anthem. Indeed, everybody sang the first verse, but the middle one … no, nobody knew that one, fortunately. I got minor applause for this, but more importantly, I could take it easy on my beer, which had become lukewarm in the meantime.

A little while later, some smart-ass thought it appropriate to call my name again. I had to face the music yet again and so I decided to turn this thing into a spectacle and earn myself a get-out-of-jail-free card for the rest of the evening. I stood on a barstool and ushered everybody to be quiet. '*Esteemed fellow-members,*' I said. '*I understand you wish me to sing yet another song. So, I would like to leave you with a choice. I could sing another meaningless cadence song, or…*' And with this I noticed the members were already backing me up. '*Or I could share with you a song, which is strictly forbidden to be sung outside of my society, the Naval Cadet Corps. You won't see anyone who knows it and tonight I would like to sing this magnificent song for you. However, I will then expect you to refrain from bothering me or calling out my name to sing any more songs. Not because I think I shouldn't have to, but because of the sacrifice I make and the respect you then display for this mighty, yet forbidden song, a song that has never ever been heard outside the Royal Naval Academy. The choice is yours.*' Everybody agreed that this was a great plan and they starting clapping and shouting. I cleared my throat once more and looked very serious, as if God himself were watching me. I assumed the position and sang three verses of the naval cadet's song aloud. It resulted in an overwhelmingly loud racket and applause and an ecstatic club thinking that I had just committed a mortal sin. They didn't need to know that naval cadets themselves took to the streets in drunken stupors, singing this song. And thus I earned my nickname. Everybody, the players, former players, injured players, they all knew who I was. I was the navy dude. Unfortunately, I failed miserably in my goal. The purpose had been no more beer, but I was yanked off my barstool anyway and everybody started pushing beer into my hands. Everybody wanted to know everything about this forbidden song, about the Naval Academy, about the military and about my rugby past. In the end, it was a long time before I made it to bed, having washed down an enormous amount of beer.

UNEXPECTED PERFORMANCE/PRESENTATION

It has probably happened to all of you at some point. You are asked to do some sort of presentation and you are not properly prepared. You are startled for a moment and then quickly recover. These presentations are only marginally about the content. In truth, it is more about the way in which you tell your story.[30] You had better make sure to catch everybody's attention. Whatever you intend to say, you must say it with flair and conviction. After all, that is what people will remember. Don't think for a minute that a couple of months down the line your audience will still know what you talked about on that one Thursday morning. What they will remember is that you were that shy person who was not fully committed to what he said. Or that you were that person who told his story with such flair, who wasn't afraid to draw attention to himself. Sure, you may add some bluff to your story, as long as you assess your audience well. If you are in a room with so-called 'subject matter experts', then use the knowledge that is present. A modest level of bluff; that is the challenge. You achieve this by assuming a fearless and self-assured attitude, but also show your vulnerable side when necessary. You may not know everything and if you are honest about that, but you can direct the conversation.

The rugby students thoroughly enjoyed having me sing a song before the entire club. Indeed, I could have done yet another one, or I could have snuck out the backdoor, or I could take control and direct the entire event. I climbed on a stool, drew all the attention to myself, gave all those present the impression they were witnessing something truly unique and ensured that I did not have to sing anymore. I was obviously lucky that I had this scenario available in my head, but this is something you control yourself, to a certain extent. You grab attention and you stand there with all the flair you are capable of displaying and then silently get off the stage again. Of course, everybody may have a bad day, but even then, you can force yourself to crawl out of your cave for a minute. After all, you have nothing to lose, only to gain!

I have seen and heard embarrassing presentations from colleagues of all nationalities. When you do a presentation, make sure that you properly address your audience and make contact with them. They will have their opinion of you ready in advance anyway. Use the knowledge that is

---

[30] T. IJzermans, L. Eckhardt - *Het woord is nu aan u!; Ontspannen spreken in het openbaar*; about speaking freely in public; Uitgeverij Thema, Zaltbommel, 2009

present in the room, speak with enthusiasm about your topic and don't hide behind a microphone or a large platform. Move around the room, ask questions, show commitment and interest. This is what you want to see when you attend a lecture given by someone else. Everybody knows you need to shrug off the first nerves. What do you have to lose? Show yourself and when you do, do it with flair!

> **Building blocks of leadership:**
> *Persuasiveness, flair*

AFGHANISTAN IN WORDS AND IMAGES

'Jochen, help,' Jean said to me. At the same time, he closed the door behind him and walked up to my desk. *'What an annoying man this Mustafa is. He simply refuses to sit at a table with me to make the presentation.'* My French colleague Jean had been asked to do a presentation about religion in Afghanistan, together with a Turkish major, Mustafa. This was one of a series of presentations in preparation of a new Afghanistan mission for my unit in Madrid. Since Afghanistan was predominantly Islamic, the presentation would mainly focus on Islam. Dos and don'ts in relation to the faith, but also the history of the Taliban, the ethnic diversity in the country and more demographic facts.

Jean expeditiously went to work and he soon found some fitting images to include in the presentation. Unfortunately, Mustafa was less enthusiastic. Jean would regularly come by my office to complain about the difficult relationship between him and Mustafa. Today, it was clear that Jean needed to get something off his chest again. He looked very frustrated. The two just couldn't click and Mustafa didn't want to start on the presentation. Jean was his military superior and he kept trying to make an appointment, but every time he did, Mustafa would come up with some excuse as why he would not be able to make it. So, Jean had made the entire presentation himself. Subsequently, a conflict arose between two people who did not understand each other, because of their cultural differences. Mustafa could not agree to tell a story about Islam, while that presentation included photographs that might be interpreted

139

negatively. That was not Islam. Jean had included pictures of an older man who married a girl not even sixteen years old and a photograph of the Taliban regime carrying out executions in a football stadium. In short, these were confrontational images and Mustafa did not want them included in his presentation. Jean didn't understand why not. These were photographs. Everybody knew this was what went on in Afghanistan. Why would you want to hide it and not tell the story? These were difficult weeks for both Jean and Mustafa, and Jean used me as an outlet. Things became so bad that Mustafa even informed the entire Turkish community about Jean's intentions.

Eventually, a Turkish officer whose additional task it was to serve as the religious leader of the Turkish community, was invited to have a look at the presentation and discuss this with Jean. In the end, the presentation was split into two parts, with Mustafa only explaining the dos and don'ts in Afghanistan. Unfortunately, this part was presented in such poor English that the English speaking audience stopped listening after a couple of minutes. Jean explained about the history of religion in Afghanistan and about the ethnic diversity. The frustrations from both sides were quite apparent, however. This was a classic example of how difficult it can sometimes be to have to work with other cultures: the lack of understanding, the lack of knowledge, but also the inability to put yourself in the other person's shoes.

Perhaps a lot less contentious, but certainly illustrative of this, was my conversation with Pedro, the doctor. Despite the fact that the Netherlands and Spain are both countries in Europe and not even that far apart, the cultural differences were enormous. When we were seated at a table, Pedro and I just could not see eye to eye. The difference with Mustafa and Jean is that they understood each other, but they refused to conform to the content. We agreed to disagree. However, in an international setting, it is useful to have some background information about the people with whom you are working.

As a leader, you need time to get used to the local customs and the international challenges. You can prepare yourself to a certain extent, but things will only fall into place when you are confronted with these situations. There are countless management blunders that show the impact of insufficient knowledge of the local culture. It has cost many businesses with highly qualified staff a pretty penny. So, all the more reason for you, as a leader, to tread softly at first, when in a strange environment and a strange culture. Make sure to be well informed by people with local knowledge. Only when you are aware of the local and cultural differences will you be able to form a proper opinion and use this to inform your management style.

> **Building blocks of leadership:**
> *Cultural awareness, people-oriented*

THE INTERNATIONAL COMMUNITY

After a thirty minute ride through the busy traffic of Kabul, I eventually reached the headquarters of the Afghanistan National Disaster Management Authority - ANDMA. This was my first visit since my arrival in Kabul, two weeks ago. Although I had said a few years back that I would not return to Afghanistan, I still took on this new challenge, far away from the Netherlands. The headquarters in Madrid provided for the majority of the occupation of the strategic headquarters of the NATO mission in Afghanistan: the International Security Assistance Forces mission, or ISAF.

The department that I worked for was involved with Governance and Development. A condition for stability in the country was *good governance*, obviously, along with a rise in certain matters of development. Think here of basic necessities such as medical provisions, education and running water. These are all non-military matters, but they are still matters that the military mission supported to a considerable extent. My task in Afghanistan was threefold. First, I was responsible for monitoring the flow of Afghan refugees to and from Pakistan and Iran. Besides this, there was support for the non-military side of the transition process. Transition was aimed specifically at the reduction of the international armed forces and handing over command to the Afghans themselves. Finally, there was the interaction with ANDMA. For example, in the case of natural disasters, ISAF would provide support to the Afghan Authority and the International Community. The international armed forces would also benefit from providing support when human lives were at stake as

141

a result of natural disasters. Stability is closely connected to this. There is often a need for specific military capacities, which the Afghans have a chronic shortage of and of which the international armed forces have plenty at their disposal. Examples include things like helicopter support, security and medical facilities.

The humanitarian international community is very keen on preserving its independence and its neutral position. This is why they consider any military involvement whatsoever as an absolute final resort. This tension area alone, between civil and military institutions in a mission territory, is an interesting environment. The people with whom I worked closely, apart from ANDMA, were staff from various UN organizations and all sorts of international organizations that preferred to see soldiers going rather than coming. In the matter of building 'good governance', they have quite valid arguments in that respect. Any military input from the international armed forces undermines the credibility and legitimacy of the Afghan government. Victims in a disaster area often see international helicopters approaching, often with huge ISAF stickers on them. These are the rescuers. This only serves to widen the gap between the population and its government. Obviously, it would be better if Afghan help were offered, as it would strengthen the position of the government and the perception of the people. My task at headquarters was to ensure that the proactive military command would not be too quick in granting support to the Afghan government and apart from this, I was also responsible for maintaining the dialogue between international actors, Afghan actors and ISAF.

AN UNEXPECTED INTERVIEW
I had an appointment with the Deputy Director of ANDMA and I had no idea what to expect. In the weeks before, in Afghanistan, I'd had one meeting after another. The United Nations, in particular, was regularly on the agenda: United Nations Development Program, United Nations office for Humanitarian Affairs, United Nations High Commissioner for Refugees. Now, finally I had another meeting with one of the Afghan partners.

I knocked on the door to the office of the Deputy Director of ANDMA. A few moments later, I was let in by a young Afghan in a leather coat. He looked as if he just got off the set of some second-rate gangster movie. In the middle of the large office, there was a huge desk, with a heavy-set man behind it. My first impression was that this was the

142

Deputy Director and I walked up to him to shake his hand. I introduced myself in my best English and the man immediately turned to his right. I had the right person in front of me indeed, but the Deputy Director did not speak a word of English and he had an interpreter next him. I looked around me and in the corner of the room, I saw two men who were responsible for providing tea. An older man was seated at a small table by the entrance that I had just walked through. However, he kept to himself. There was a young boy as well, sitting on a couch, quietly staring ahead. Judging from the purse that he had with him and his effeminate appearance, also the manner in which he sat on the bench, I presumed that this might just be an 'intimate acquaintance' of the Deputy Director. This was not uncommon for someone of his stature, as I had once been informed.

The interpreter asked me to take a seat on the couch. The Deputy Director also made his way to the seating area and sat down next to the interpreter. After two cups of tea and exchanging a few pleasantries, I was ready to leave. I stood up and wanted to shake hands with the Deputy Director. At that moment, the 'intimate acquaintance' got up as well, pulled a microphone from his handbag, turned a couple of buttons and before I knew it, the microphone was shoved under my nose and I was asked what ISAF intended to do for the people who were stranded by an enormous flood in the north of the country, where, earlier that afternoon, dozens of people had died...

For a second there, I was disconcerted. I never expected the 'intimate acquaintance' to be a journalist. I also had not yet heard of any major disaster that had taken place in my area of responsibility and I was literally overwhelmed by the microphone that was held under my nose. A second later, I came to grips with myself again and I disregarded the microphone and the interviewer. I turned to the Deputy Director and thanked him kindly for his time. Then I turned back to the journalist, who was no longer sure whether or not he should continue to hold the microphone under my nose, and told him that he surprised me with this disaster and that I found it heart-breaking news that so many Afghans had died, as he claimed. I expressed my deepest sympathies for the victims and their families. I also presumed the Afghan government would act vigorously and would certainly be capable of providing first aid. If so requested, ISAF would most certainly provide support in external cases. I remembered my lessons in communication, 'how to deal with the press' from a couple of years earlier. In the end, you, as the interviewee, are the one to decide whether you make use of this free publicity or not. The victims and their surviving relatives always have first priority in the message you wish to convey. In the few seconds that it took me to thank the Deputy Director, I had found the time to quickly think about this. Also, the general message was clear. The Afghans are well capable of taking action themselves. Following my general message, I referred him to our press representatives for further information. I thanked everyone again and walked out the door. I could tell that my Afghan partners would have preferred a different answer.

When you are confronted with a journalist who wants to interview you, make sure that you prepare well, if you have the time for this. Others may also suddenly approach you in order to draw a statement from you. Here as well, the rule of thumb is careful preparation. Make sure that you know what this conversation is about, what the purpose is and who gave the order.[31] This will provide you with an idea of the questions you may expect. They will be attuned to a target group. Also, make sure that you control the direction of the interview; after all, you are the one determining which message you convey. This may also mean not allowing yourself to be lured into giving an interview. Finally, you can also make proper arrangements for the end result. Obviously, it would be ideal if you had the time and opportunity to review the story and check it for errors. Don't forget that you lead the conversation; you determine how you will be using this free publicity. Stick to your message and only say things that are relevant and of which you are certain. This is where we refer back to the four elements of communication presented in a preceding chapter: quantity, quality, relation and style. And whatever happens, remain calm and polite at all times. In the end, this can only benefit your message.

THE POLITICIANS' WAY
A new environment, far away from home, with other colleagues, working in a new field and in a culture not your own. All these elements are reason enough to first see how matters pan out. Unfortunately, you don't always have time for this. Especially not on a mission like this one in Afghanistan. You are expected to get onboard immediately. In general, you will only be posted here for six months to a year. If you really want

---

[31] S. Piët - *Het Groot Communicatiedenkboek* - a new look into communication; Pearson Benelux, Amsterdam, 2005

to accomplish something in that time, you won't be able to familiarize yourself with the task at hand. Everybody expects something from you: your colleagues in your own working environment, the Afghan partners and the international partners.

The strategic headquarters had every interest in maintaining good relations. This meant that I had to do a lot of talking with these partners. Say the right things, but also refrain from saying too many things. Don't make promises you can't keep, think fast, switch fast and always consider the relationship. And be sure to make clear what your interests are. In all of my conversations with Afghans, I have always been fully aware that I often conveyed the same message. 'ISAF is certainly prepared to render assistance, if both the Afghan authorities and the United Nations request such, but you are responsible for the first actions yourself. You and your ministries will need to take up action as soon as possible to prevent or reduce unnecessary human suffering.'

Still, every time, I felt as if the message did not come across. Every time, the same arguments were mentioned, the same questions were asked. Isn't ISAF present with a great deal of helicopters? Doesn't the western world have the money to help? You are not here just to observe, are you? It was precisely these situations that I should use to negotiate. Not so much negotiate the price of a product, but rather to maintain the relationship, to get the Afghans to work and leave a positive image of ISAF behind. In the conversations with the Afghans, the relationship is very important, especially where a man of stature is concerned, like the Deputy Director, who is always right.

A well-known method of negotiation is the so-called 'politicians' method.'[32] This method specifically aims at dealing with unexpected requests. One of the most important aspects of this is to listen to the request very intently. Do not interrupt the person making the request; do not engage in a discussion, but try to delay some specific details. Of course, you can always answer, without obligation, by pointing out that you will look into the situation. Also asking for additional motivation, or simply continuing to ask follow-up questions to find out more, will work excellently and will give you extra time to think. In Afghanistan, however, the relationship comes first. As a rule, I would say that my

---

[32] H.C. Altmann - *Overtuigen; een kunst die je kunt leren*; about convincing and how to learn it; MVG-verlag, Landsberg am Lech, Germany

conversation partner was right, but ... there's always something like 'however', 'but' or 'let's not forget'. Ideal words to both clearly bring your message across as well as to say to your conversation partner that he's right. This diplomatic trait and manner of negotiation is a condition for leaders acting within a political force field. In many leading positions, there is always a political force field.

Of course, you must remain vigorous in the discussion. Acknowledging that your conversation partner is right, merely for the sake of maintaining the relationship, is not of much use. First, you undermine yourself when you do this and, besides, nothing constructive will come of it. As a leader, you are expected to be constructive. Based on your negotiation skills and communication skills, you should be perfectly capable of finding a balance.

> **Building blocks of leadership:**
> *Negotiation skills, communication skills, diplomacy*

HIERARCHICAL STRUCTURES

'I think that as a department, we need to approach some things more positively and not reject every job, wondering if nobody else can do it. I think we have plenty of capacity left,' I said to the head of the department. He was taken aback by this a bit. He had not expected it when I asked him if he had 'a moment' for me. Usually this is not the most sensible manner of talking to a military superior. Especially when he has a Spanish military background and considers rank and stature as essential elements of leadership. I was also aware of the difference in perception over power distance, but I had chosen my words delicately and had kept it fairly mild. After working at the headquarters for a couple of months, everybody was aware of how things were done around here. The Spanish lieutenant colonel may have been the head of the department, but in practice, he really was there just for decorative reasons. This was also a huge frustration for his superiors. We really were on entirely different wavelengths, but despite his negative attitude, I tried to make it work somehow.

Unfortunately, the Spanish chief took things far too lightly. The good man would come in through the back door so that nobody would notice that he came in late every morning. Most of the time, after having scanned his e-mails, he would be picked up by a Spanish colleague to go for breakfast. Others had breakfast before going to their work. At some point, later in the morning, all the Spaniards would go for coffee for an hour and then they went for lunch at half past twelve, which was the sign for my boss to start on his siesta. Most of the time he would return to the office around four o'clock. This was around the time that I would go work out at the gym, so we wouldn't see each other until after dinner. Often, he would only return to the office to phone Spain. The working hours at an international headquarters in a mission area are often longer than what we are used to at home. There are no weekends and, in general, the normal routine was to work from very early in the morning to very late at night. Unfortunately, my Spanish boss was more involved with his own schedule. When he was in the office, he would mainly have a negative attitude and pass on work to others, making sure that he did not overextend himself, and he was always trying to leave without a sound.

The reason that I pointed out to my Spanish colleague that the department might be viewed in a negative light for its willingness to pass on work to others, was because he had just told a new colleague in our department that he did not want her to take on certain additional tasks. This female lieutenant colonel from Croatia, Andrea, wanted to work more than anything, because she'd been in the office for two weeks and she'd had little else to do but read through some documents and hope for some direction from him. Neither of them was very comfortable in English and she was not capable of explaining clearly to him why she thought she could do with some extra work. Nor did he allow her too much say in the matter.

As soon as I had asked to speak with him, I knew that it was not going to go well. I had phrased my statement neatly and politely, but he was the Spanish head of the department. 'How dare he?' I saw him thinking. His face turned red and he started to stutter that I could keep my opinion to myself and that he would gladly tell me what he thought of me. By now, our conversation could also be heard by others. I paused for a moment, but I continued the discussion. I calmly told him, in a somewhat muted voice and with arguments, why it would make sense to have Andrea take on extra work. I could sense that everybody was listening in and

I purposely kept my composure and remained prudent in my choice of words, continuously addressing him by his rank. He was pulled entirely out of his comfort zone and he didn't know how to react. In the spur of the moment, he aimed the discussion towards me and he accused me of not keeping him informed about my work activities.

I chose carefully my words, thinking about all of the relationships that were at stake here, about his relationship within the hierarchical structures of the headquarters, and about the fact that others were most certainly listening. I decided to keep my opinion to myself and bring up this discussion again later. However, the fact that I did not react, made him turn from red to crimson and he started shouting at me that he was the boss here and he was the one who determined how the work should be done. He forgot that everybody else could hear us. He probably used that moment to assert his authority. Our one-on-one moment, as I had envisaged it, had clearly failed. I thought to myself, "Leadership is not something you can claim, you have to earn it." I decided to keep that thought to myself, however. He had made a complete fool of himself. On the one hand, he did this by screaming loudly that he was the boss and everybody had to answer to him. On the other hand, he did it by suddenly claiming his leadership after months of being unproductive. The Spanish lieutenant colonel mumbled something in Spanish and angrily stormed out of the office.

STILL A LOSER

I had chosen my words carefully. Not because I was looking for a confrontation, but because I was committed to the result I was seeking and I wanted to set up something worthwhile here. That is no easy task if you have a boss who wants to work as little as possible, who is mainly negative and who prefers to drag all his staff into that negativity with him. Our discussion was a perfect display of how things had gone up to that point. A cursing and raging Spaniard storming out of his office with a thick red neck, in search of coffee. Normally, he was cursing and raging about all the work that accidentally came his way and that he had to pass on to others. This time he was cursing and raging because of an annoying Dutch naval officer. Andrea did not know what to do and she sat quietly in a corner. I had spoken to my Spanish boss separately and approached him openly and extremely politely and I had told him in all honesty what I thought of the situation and how we might improve it. When I did this, I purposely didn't address his own contribution, but in particular pointed out the opportunities for the department. Somehow, I knew he did not want to hear it. After all, he was the head of the department. We already had cultural differences, we thought differently about leadership and about work and now, I had dared to try to steer him in a certain direction.

Generally, communication will be more effective as the cultural similarity between conversation partners increases.[33] This also applies to the knowledge and cultural background of your conversation partner. We clearly had very little effective communication between us. I could have let it all be, but since I didn't feel like staring blankly ahead me for seven months and I actually wanted to do something worthwhile, I had decided to confront the boss, or rather, the department, with the apparent negativity and passing on of work. Managing-up goes further than merely creating a good relationship with your boss, however. Especially if this hierarchical relationship is only for a short while. What you do need to realize is you have not been able to turn the tide as you wanted and failed to win over the boss. In addition, your resilience clearly has its limits. No matter how you look at it, you will lose again, but sometimes a loss is calculated and you take one step back in order to go two steps forward.

> **Building blocks of leadership:**
> *Ambition, managing up, resilience.*

---

[33] W. Shadid - *Culturele diversiteit en interculturele communicatie; Verschenen in Veghel, H. van: Waarden onder de meetlat; Het Europese waardenonderzoek in discussie* – about cultural diversity and intercultural communication; Damon bv, Budel, 2002

THE ATTACK

Just as I drove away from the base to attend a meeting in the center of Kabul, I heard a huge explosion behind the gate. The ground was shaking under my feet. A few seconds later, I could hear gunshots and several smaller explosions. I immediately realized that I would not make it to the planned meeting with my Afghan colleagues. Indeed, as the driver turned the car around and headed for the parking lot, the camp alarm sounded. 'Camp lockdown, camp lockdown,' sounded through the speakers. I took my stuff from the car and decided to walk back to my workplace. As I walked back, I was surprised at the severity and proximity of the battle. I could hear guns rattling from multiple sides.

Back at the office, I encountered some mild panic. Andrea was staring ahead and told me this reminded her of the war of the Balkans some years before. I could not imagine what she must have been through. However, my American colleague from the Rule of Law Department, was the most taken aback. The fear was clearly visible in his eyes. I decided to leave my computer as it was and sit across from him to keep his mind off all the misery that was unfolding outside the gate.

This American colonel, David, was head of the Rule of Law Department. In his regular life, he was a lawyer, but since he was in the reserves, there was the possibility of him to be called up to serve in the military. This is how he suddenly ended up in Afghanistan, in uniform. He had two captains working for him in his department. They were young lawyers who usually worked at the Judge Advocate General unit of the American army, back in the United States.

From the beginning of my deployment, it was clear that David enjoyed holding people accountable for the things they said and he liked to challenge almost anything. He had no sense of maintaining relationships at all, which was probably because of his background. He would literally challenge everything openly. We got together every weekend with the governance department to discuss what had transpired during the week and what the coming period had in store and every week there would be discussions between the Icelandic director of the governance department, a French colonel who was acting director and David. He would sit, slumped in his chair and annoy the hell out of them. It was quite obvious that the French colonel did not appreciate this one bit. After the meeting, I often walked back to the office with the Americans and the entire discussion would be repeated all over again with the young captains listening to David muttering. He was not one to keep his opinions to himself and he would drag his two young disciples with him into his barrage of complaints.

Often, after a heated discussion, a wrongly interpreted e-mail or phone call, David would use his two young captains as a sounding board to confirm how wrong the other party was. David was a smooth talker, a quick thinker and he always had his opinion ready to be pronounced openly, without considering his relationship with the other party.

Unfortunately, his boys, the two military lawyers, were so impressed by his attitude that they were copying his behavior. They would drop statements left and right about matters that were not handled properly by others. They would even criticize high officers with whom David did not have a good relationship. Thus, I noticed how David's negativity towards others had its effect on the two young captains as well.

Now that there was such heavy fighting outside the gate and the colonel was shaking like a leaf in his chair, the image that the two captains had of their leader had suddenly changed entirely. Later on, one of the captains even told me that David really should have stayed in the US, because he was unfit to lead under such circumstances.

Apparently, David himself also doubted his approach towards leadership. While we were sitting at his desk, we discussed the matter of leadership extensively. He felt that it was perfectly fine for his two captains to know what he thought and felt. He tried to let them grow quickly and let them think about what they did, without considering the hierarchy too much. I asked him how they would perceive this. After all, they are soldiers and that is how they are assessed. Thinking for yourself is important and positive criticism has nothing to do with rank and class but it is still about the way you criticize. He leaned back and pondered this. His thoughts were no longer with the battle that was going on in the background.

At that moment, a mortar grenade struck very close to us. There was a huge explosion that made David jump so high that he almost touched the ceiling. Our conversation was clearly over. The loud bang made David crawl under his desk and all my efforts to calm him down had become undone.

THROW IN THE TOWEL

As a leader, you have to be aware of what you say. David enjoyed challenging people for what they said, to get under their skin and most often to point out to military superiors that they were wrong in a tactless manner. He would regularly involve the two young captains in these fights.

I found it interesting that the two captains could not appreciate this anymore after the battle. At first, they copied David's behavior, but after a while, they developed an aversion to him. Where the lawyer expected to gain their respect, the opposite was effected. He caused himself to lose face because he was always running down others. Our lawyer thought himself to be lord and master, particularly verbally, in his own language.

David forgot that the French colonel, who was acting director, had served on active duty in Africa for over twenty years as a marine and he did not exactly warm to the pretty phrases used by the lawyer. Despite his frustration, the French colonel always took the honorable way out and he never lost face. In the end, he gained the respect from the men. Not by being the nicest or the funniest, but by his way of acting and by not reacting. David indicated that he found leadership important. Still, it was clear soon enough that he was not a born and bred leader. He had a strong opinion, which he shared with his colleagues any time he saw fit. He was a dominant presence, always ready to speak his mind and often unable to keep his big mouth shut. He was also not much of a diplomat. To him, it was all about letting his opinion be known, without wondering how this came across to recipients or audiences. However, what was peculiar was that David was all in favor of the development of his staff. He wanted them to think for themselves, make decisions on their own and not approach the hierarchical aspects too seriously. It was exactly his style of leadership, however, that caused the opposite effect on his staff.

In the moments when things got really tense, David was nowhere to be found. Perhaps it would be better for him to throw in the towel, hang his uniform in the closet and put on a tailored three-piece suit or judge's robe.

> **Building blocks of leadership:**
> *Exemplary behavior, tact, calm*

8. LEARNING FROM OTHERS

A wise man learns from his mistakes, but only a wiser man learns from others
-Old Chinese proverb-

In an organization like the Defense Department, everybody has stories of good and bad leadership. In a hierarchical organization with so many layers, everybody is managed and there are many leaders. It would be a missed opportunity, not to learn from these stories.

BACK FROM THE MISSION
'Can I have two beers please, madam?' I asked the friendly lady serving drinks at the outdoor café in Haarlem. It was the first really nice day of spring. Everybody was walking around the city, showing off just a bit too much skin. The outdoor cafés on the central square actually weren't ready for so much sun yet and their staffs had totally lost their knack for serving outdoors after the long, dark winter months. It didn't really matter, though. Maarten and I were finally sitting here again and it was great. Ever since he became a submarine commander, he had not been home very often. After a long mission of several months for him and my mission in Afghanistan, we were lucky enough to be able to enjoy the first rays of spring together and take pleasure in the smaller things that make life so beautiful.

Maarten had opted for submarine service a long time ago. Together with another friend of ours, Piet, he went through all the ranks onboard the 'cigar' and eventually become eligible for the commander training. Not too long ago, we sat enjoying a beer and celebrating Maarten's successful completion of commander training. He had done it, but Piet had not...

SUBMARINE COMMANDER SCHOOL
After their initial education at the Royal Naval Academy, Piet and Maarten both chose to continue their careers in the submarine service. This unit of the Royal Navy is a small, but very professional unit that demands the most of its people. After all, it is no small task to spend weeks under water with fifty men in bizarre, challenging and even dangerous circumstances. The men had very limited living space. Beds

153

were regularly shared by different divisions so it was not all that strange to get into a bed that someone else just got out of. Privacy on board a submarine is non-existent and the staff is expected to have a high level of tolerance and social adaptation.

The Walrus-class submarine.

The Dutch submarine of the type Walrus-class is a diesel-electric submarine. Small, agile and silent. Especially the 'silent' aspect is vital for the submarine service, because in current operations Dutch submarines are mainly used to gather intelligence. They are the eyes and ears in territories where you don't wish to be found, but of which you do want to know more, for the purposes of international security. Opting for the submarine service after your Naval Academy training carries quite the risk. It means you will have to go through all the officers' positions on board of a submarine first, before you reach the final hurdle: submarine commanders' training. If you successfully complete this training, you may call yourself a submarine commander and at a relatively young age, you will be in charge of a sub and its crew. You will hold the rank of lieutenant commander. This is a role not held by many.

Dutch submarine commander training is one of the toughest naval training courses in the world. Other countries try to gain access to this

Dutch course for their future commanders. The course is given each year, with only one or two Dutch nationals participating. The structure of the training consists of a lot of theoretical knowledge. It also includes many lessons on a simulated submarine bridge on which everything is simulated by the computer. In short, you learn how to navigate and sail safely, something the men have been doing for years while holding all sorts of different positions. After this, you are expected to actually deploy the ship surrounded by other ships around that have it in for you. It is, therefore, no strange sight to see a submarine commander with multiple stop watches hanging around his neck. He uses these in determining the course and speed of the ships around you, all the while calculating how much time he has left before he must make his sub dive in order to safely sail underneath the other ships. When is it safe to deploy weapon's systems? There is a lot of mental arithmetic, setting the right priorities based on analytical capacity and making the right decisions when it matters. Before starting on this training course, the men already know how to sail a ship, they are good at mental arithmetic and they know the entire ship and all its systems inside and out. During commander training, they are observed to see what their limitations are, how they react to information overload and to lack of sleep, while still managing to safely command the ship with maximum exploitation of the capacities, under severe circumstances.

Piet and Maarten both idolized the submarine service. After years of all sorts of different positions, they were finally allowed to start on that last hurdle. I tried to assess their chances of success in advance. Piet was the one who was best at studying. He was a pretty smart guy. He sailed through his studies with ease and, in terms of knowledge, nobody could beat him. His difficulty, however, was that he often seemed unsure of himself and was always seeking confirmation that he was doing things properly.

Maarten, on the other hand, is much more impulsive. He is a big man who has to work hard and think hard to get things right. His strength is that men are prepared to work for him. 'No Nonsense' is what he lives by. As I saw it, I believed only one of them would succeed in completing the course. I thought Piet's analytical capacity would be the determining factor. Piet would think things through just that little bit more.

They started on their training with energy and enthusiasm. The pressure was raised every time and Maarten's learning curve clearly took a much steeper flight than his fellow course members' did. At the start of the course, Maarten had serious doubts as to whether or not he would be able to it. He dug deep, however, worked harder, performed better and as the weeks went by, his results improved, while Piet's declined. Piet became uncertain and looked, with increasing urgency, for confirmation from instructors and supervisors. Meanwhile, the men got more information to process and everything became more complex by the day. In the final weeks of training, the course members were put on a real submarine. For three weeks, they would push the ship to its limits under all sorts of circumstances. The time of 'a little bit of mental arithmetic' was far behind them. It was all about the total picture now.

The remaining course members would take turns in commanding the ship. The assessors were present 24/7 to monitor everything and give their opinion. And it was all real. You had real ships sailing around you, there were real shallow parts, real crews and a real submarine at your disposal. The smallest of errors could have fatal consequences. As the end of the training drew near, fewer errors were tolerated. Those who still made errors at this stage of the training course would be relieved from their temporary command, the ship would rise to the surface and a helicopter would fly to the submarine from England to take you off board. This would be the last time you would be onboard an operational submarine. After all these years of commitment to the submarine service, this was really the end of the line. You had failed. The men were purposely driven to their absolute limits and tested fully. After weeks of hardly any sleep, you were still required every day to set the right priorities and dare to make decisions; to know your own limits, but also the limits of the ship and crew that you had been entrusted with.

And then it happened… During the last week, Piet had command of the submarine and he made an error in judgment. He made a wrong, yet not fatal decision. He could not let this go. The exhaustion combined with the stress of situation kept him from being able to pull himself together and gain control of the situation. He was disappointed and followed every error with a new error. He hung his head and continued to be visibly disappointed about that one wrong decision. His indecisiveness and doubts immediately affected the crew as well. 'Where is the leader?' they wondered. Piet thought too much about certain options and errors that had been made instead of forcing himself to make a decision and get over his mistake. This was the end of Piet's submarine career.

Maarten, on the other hand, fought his way through the course and set priorities at the right time. He got the best out of his crew and out of himself. His power – as opposed to Piet – was that Maarten kept his head up and he aimed to conquer every situation. You never give up in front of the troops. Maybe he didn't control everything and maybe he got lucky in certain situations, but the main thing was he emanated leadership at all times. He was an example to the fifty men who were looking to him as their commander: the man who never gives up, who knows when to set priorities and when decisions need to be made - even if you're not sure and you have to base your decisions on a gut feeling.

Not long after Piet had hung his head, the submarine was brought to the surface and the helicopter was circling above the deck to take him to the coast. A couple of days later, Maarten also left the ship, but he did so in Plymouth Harbour, in England, as new submarine commander of the Dutch Navy.

> **Building blocks of leadership:**
> *Ability to prioritize, decisiveness, go-getter*

So Maarten and I sat at the central square in Haarlem, enjoying a beer. For Maarten, the commander course seemed like ages ago, since he had just finished a magnificent mission as commander, with his team and his ship out to sea, independently 'taking care of a job'. I was obviously anxious to hear about his leadership experiences and the challenges he faced as a commander. After all, it is no small feat to get a ship like this to carry out a secret mission, at such a young age. Even the family back home often does not know where their dear husband or daddy is located. In those months, Maarten had seen quite a lot. He started to tell his story.

INFECTION IN PORT

We had just finished our weekend in port. Most of the crew members had sent for their partners and had used the weekend to relax. After all, half the journey had been completed. Obviously, there were plenty of men who had not sent for their partners and they were enjoying a good time in the many hotels and clubs around the city. On Sunday afternoon, right after I had dropped my wife at the airport for her flight back to the Netherlands, I was looking at the naval maps for the following mission and there was a knock on the door of my cabin. It was the medic. He was my only medical expert and support on board for minor inconveniences, first aid and possibly, to stabilize an injured person: a crewmember you cannot do without. However, when there are serious accidents, you must get medical specialists as soon as possible, which is all the more difficult when you are secretly operating in an area where you are not exactly supposed to be.

'Commander,' the medic said, *'we have a small problem. One of the sailors has a minor infection on his testicles. I think it would be wise to have it looked at.'* I was not too keen on the idea of going to a strange hospital on a Sunday afternoon in a foreign port. This was one of our technical crewmembers; it's not like I have them available in abundance. I was already contemplating whether I would take him along or not. I decided not to worry about it before I heard what the doctor had to say.

Late in the evening, the medic and the sailor returned. The hospital had prescribed antibiotics and instructions to keep everything clean. I decided to contact the Netherlands just to make sure it was okay for me to go under with this sailor on board for such a long mission. After consulting with a physician from defense headquarters in the Netherlands and having a conversation with the medic and sailor, everybody agreed that it would be no problem to depart with him on board.

After a short night, we headed out to sea. We went under shortly after we had left, not to rise to the surface again for several weeks. At least, that was our intention. The lights on the ship gradually turned red, the sounds were limited to a minimum and slowly, but surely, the ship moved towards territories where this Dutch cigar did not belong.

At the end of the first day, a slightly worried medic came to my cabin. *'Commander, our sailor is not doing too well after all, I'm afraid,'* he said, sounding a bit nervous. *'What do you mean?'* I asked. This was not something I wanted to hear. I had taken every step to convince myself that it was okay to take this sailor along on the mission. Now, not even twenty-four hours into the mission and the first setback had already presented itself. *'I'm monitoring him sir, but he maintains a mild fever.'* I thanked the medic for his report, obviously fully trusting all would end well. The first two days went by. I had almost put this testicle issue out of my mind and I decided to go to bed on time. I went for one last round on the bridge, checked the maps and had a brief conversation with the officer of the watch. I was reassured and decided that it was time for bed.

AS BIG AS MY HEAD

'Commander,' I heard a voice somewhere in my subconscious and at the same time, I felt a powerful hand pulling my body straight. *'Commander,'* I heard a painful panic in my ear. I was wide-awake in an instant, staring into the bloodshot eyes of my sailor from Operations. *'We have to surface sir, NOW! I can't stand it anymore!'* The sailor was groaning in pain: *'Commander, bring the ship up NOW and take me to a hospital!'* The sweat was dripping from his forehead and I could tell he was in tremendous pain. Unfortunately, I was in the middle of an operation and I could not possibly surface the ship here. The sailor bent over my bunk and leaned on my pillow as I phoned the bridge. *'Commander speaking, get the medic to my cabin. NOW!'* I hung up, secure in the knowledge that the urgency in my voice would set the wheels in motion.

Not a minute later, the medic was in my cabin. The sailor had totally lost it. He did not care what would happen, but this ship had to come out of the water and he had to be flown to a hospital immediately. Normally, I can deal with it just fine when somebody is stressed out and in pain but this was a 6'6" sailor, covered in tattoos and an active 'free fighter' (in mixed martial arts: MMA). Somehow, there was a lot more urgency in his words than there would have been in the average crewmember. At the request of the medic, the sailor dropped his pants and I almost jumped out of my own in shock. His testicle was the size of my head and in all the colors of the rainbow too. The sailor firmly repeated his words when he saw our shocked reactions. That was probably not our wisest move. It would have been better to react coolly, saying that it wasn't that bad. We inadvertently confirmed to him that this had to be serious, however, in the way that we reacted.

I had to think quickly. Steering the ship to the surface was impossible. Having the sailor walk around like that – not a chance. In my mind, I cursed the hospital in the port we left, but also the physician in the Netherlands who had guaranteed me that this would not jeopardize the mission. While the sailor was cursing and raging about wanting to strangle people, I opened my safe. I had a leather case in it with a few last resorts to fall back on. I took out a valium pen from the case, walked over to the sailor and stuck the pen in his leg. He dropped like a sack of flour. I pulled two crewmembers from the command center and ordered them to pick up the giant and put him in the officer's cabin. I ordered the medic to keep watch over him at all times and to do everything he could to control his pain.

I walked to the command center and considered my options. I knew that I did not want to have this sailor on board for too long, so thinking hard, I decided to pull away to open sea under water. I knew an American fleet was practicing somewhere in the vicinity. This was a possibility for me to send the sailor quickly and safely back to the port. While he was lying in bed hallucinating and the medic was worried for his well-being, the ship was slowly moving in the direction of our American friends.

ON THE LAMP
Tick, tick, tick, the lamp clicked. I had risen to the surface and was sailing next to one of the American naval supply ships. The radioman, responsible for all communications on board, was standing next to me on the fin of our sub. The night was clear and the weather was calm. The ship cut through the water almost noiselessly and we watched the waves drop from the sides a couple of meters below us. The radioman flashed the signal to the big supply ship and received some flashes back a couple of minutes later. '*Message,*' I dictated. '*This is Dutch submarine U888, stop ... On a mission, stop ... Patient on board, stop ... Request medevac by boat, stop*' ... It remained silent from the other side. Then, '*Standby,*' came from the huge bridge. Obviously, I knew exactly what was going on. This ship had started in formation and had sailed into the night along with others. Nobody had seen the Dutch submarine come alongside and then all of a sudden, unexpectedly, you have this U-boat signaling you, waking up large parts of your crew.

We watched the ship quickly coming to life. The lamp from the high bridge a couple of hundred yards away started signaling again: '*Reduce speed to five knots... stop,'* was the signal. Then a light was switched on at the side of the tanker and a small boat was lowered into the water. Before we knew it, two American doctors climbed on board our submarine. I felt a huge wave of relief. I knew our presence in this area was still unknown since we had only used light signals for communication. Any form of radio traffic would have meant the end of our mission. Now I also had two doctors on board and I was certain they would take my sailor with them to the supply ship. The medical facilities of our NATO friend were of similar quality to a Dutch hospital. Indeed, not long afterward, the sailor was strapped to a stretcher and lifted into the small boat alongside our submarine. As they sped away with the patient and the two doctors, we exchanged some formalities with the signaling lamp and before the sailor was onboard the tanker, my ship resumed its mission.

Maarten and I had finished our beers and the sun had slowly disappeared behind the buildings. I was impressed with his story about leadership. Long after we had left the café and said goodbye, this story of the sailor continued to play in my mind.

Building blocks of leadership:
Decisiveness, ability to prioritize

Maarten's story proves that sometimes, usually in unexpected situations, you have to make sudden decisions for which you cannot possibly train. Every leader is faced with decisions, for which he has not been educated. In such situations, it is key to think and to act quickly, but also to set the right priorities for yourself. Only then can you make a decision. This may be a decision that will not win you any popularity contests, but you have to stand by your decision and emanate that as well. Later, when the time is right, you can explain why you made the decision. It is possible you will gain support then. If not, so be it! This is why you became a leader.

COLLECTING BUILDING BLOCKS

All the stories from the preceding chapters contain the building blocks of leadership; building blocks in all shapes and sizes. Building blocks in the form of a noun or an adjective and of the verb *to have* or *to be*. The blocks in themselves do not stand for much. In Part II of this book, I will look further into the concept of leadership and I will explore which building blocks are of real significance in the leadership model. Part I has provided you with a nice framework about good and bad leaders, now it is time to make all of this information useful for you as a leader!

PART II

THE THEORY

9. A REFERENCE FRAMEWORK FOR LEADERSHIP

To know what one knows and to know what one does not know: that is knowledge.
-Confucius- (551-479 BC)

The stories in Part I contained examples of both good and bad leadership. It is obvious that leadership is not something you pick up just like that. Knowledge and experience are essential elements of leadership. Besides this, character and personality play an important role. Fortunately, being able to lead properly is something that can be learned and in this second part of the book, I would like to lend a hand with that.

What is leadership? Am I a good leader? How can I provide better leadership? At first glance, these seem like fairly easy questions. That is, until you try to answer them. The longer you think about them, the more questions they will trigger. At the end of this chapter, you will have gained more insight in the topic of leadership and you will be able to partially answer the questions above.

WHAT IS LEADERSHIP?
We would like to be able to see a reflection of our actions and receive some sort of confirmation that things are going well. When things are not going well, we want to have the tools to get a grip on the situation again. We obviously also like to read about leadership in order to improve ourselves, to develop and gather inspiration. There are several models that may help you to determine what type of leader you are, which form of leadership you can apply and what characteristics a good leader needs. You may have one or two books by renowned authors like Covey, Quinn and Hersey on your bookshelf, or perhaps you've read some of their work. One obvious reason why books about leadership are popular is that they provide a framework for leadership.

Some famous authors have defined the concept of leadership as follows:

'Leadership is communicating to people their worth and potential so clearly that they come to see it in themselves.' (Stephen Covey)[34]

'Leadership is a fundamental state where people are results centered, internally directed, other focused and externally open.' (Robert Quinn)[35]

'Leadership (leading) is every attempt to influence the behavior of another individual or a group.' (Paul Hersey)[36]

What do these definitions tell us? How do you know if you are a good leader? In any case, you are not a leader just because you believe you are. You are also not a leader because you were hired to fill a top position in an organization. You are a leader because you justify your leadership towards others. It is exactly that 'third' person, the other, who is the common denominator in the three definitions above. The ability to ensure that others acknowledge you as leader is what I believe leadership to be. My definition of leadership is as follows:

'Leadership is the ability to ensure that others acknowledge you as a leader by, wittingly or unwittingly, applying specific (leadership) features.'

Ensuring that others acknowledge you as a leader is where the real challenge lies. You only need to apply the right features, at the right time, in the right way.

Therefore, the leader does not influence the behavior of the other just like that, wittingly or unwittingly under the banner of leadership. In Hersey's definition, every attempt to influence the behavior of an individual or group is branded as leading. According to Hersey, situational leadership is the ability to switch between direction and support, depending on the job competence, the ability and the willingness of the employee.

---

[34] S.R. Covey - *De 7 eigenschappen van effectief leiderschap* - translation of The 7 habits of highly effective people; Uitgeverij Business Contact, Amsterdam, 2007

[35] R.E. Quinn - Building the bridge as you walk on it; a guide for leading change; John Wiley & Sons, Jossey-Bass, San Francisco, 2004

[36] P. Hersey - *Situationeel leiding geven* - A practical model to flexibly respond to changing circumstances; Business Contact, Amsterdam, 2008

However, there are some justifiable criticisms to the Hersey model,[37] the most important of which is the basic principle of situational leadership. The model points out which behavior a leader should display to be effective in view of the professional competence and dedication of the employee. Leadership is more than that, however. Leadership also means a course is set and the leader gets his people to follow it. In short, the leader shows vision and decisiveness. What is distinctive in the approach to leadership in this book is the simplicity of the model and the focus on yourself. After all, you are the one who is supposed to lead; others will not do that for you!

THE UNWITTINGLY SKILLED LEADER

How do I know which specific traits I need to deploy to justify myself as a leader? In other words, what causes people to accept me as a leader? Isn't it true that as the level of leadership changes, a different performance is required? The chairman of the local sports club will probably lead a group of volunteers in a different way than the general manager of a company listed on the stock exchange will lead his employees.

Most characteristics of leadership develop through individual growth of knowledge, experience, character and personality. The total of the level of available knowledge and gained experiences, but also the character and personality that typify you, are an indication of the chances that you will justify your leadership. Actual justification of leadership is difficult to measure and may be different in every situation, even when the same people surround you

There are a number of characteristics that we often see in generally acknowledged leaders. I refer to the most important of these as 'Key Leadership Features'. Experienced leaders intuitively sense how they can use key leadership features in certain situations or with certain people.

THE KEY LEADERSHIP FEATURES; KLF

The building blocks from the preceding chapters obviously are not all key features of good leadership. It is also different for every organization. At

---

[37] Drs. S. Dalenberg, Prof. Dr. A.L.W. Vogelaar - *Leiderschapsvisie: theorie en praktijk; Een beschouwing van de visies op leiderschap binnen Defensie* - an analysis of the visions on leadership within the department of Defense; *Militaire Spectator* - a military scientific magazine for the Dutch armed forces; volume 181, number 5, 2012

certain moments, the objectives you aim for, the external influence on your situation, the people that you lead and your individual characteristics are those key features. As a leader, you must be able to switch between the right features, while maintaining awareness of the variables in your specific situation. This will be clarified in the next chapter.

For the leadership model, we use the relevant building blocks from the preceding chapters. By stacking them up in a logical order, a cluster of certain leadership features will arise. We look at the common features of the building blocks, for example, the cluster social skills, mental aspects or influencing the behavior of others and this cluster of blocks together forms the Key Leadership Features (KLFs). The building blocks in a cluster can be subdivided in blocks of 'to have' and blocks of 'to be'. You may be decisive (a 'to be' building block) and you have charisma (a 'to have' building block). This cluster leads to the following building model:

Figure 2: Building blocks of leadership

From the above figure we can draw up the 'Key Leadership Features' or KLFs. These are:

• Social features
• Observed features
• Action features
• Diplomatic features
• Mental features
• Guiding features

The pallet of KLFs enables you to adapt your leadership behavior to your environment, like the mixer on a stereo. A bit more bass, a little less treble, pump up the volume or turn it down, you determine which buttons you turn yourself. You do not do this randomly. You look at your surroundings for this. How large is the room, how are the acoustics, how many people are inside and where are the speakers positioned? Every environment, or even the same environment, but with different characteristics, will demand the unique settings of your mixer. It is the same with leadership. Every situation is different; every audience is different and even if you have the same audience, they may react differently.

However, if your mixer contains twenty different buttons, it will be hard to find the right setting for that special situation. This also applies to 'leadership settings'. It is impossible to find the right settings for all the building blocks from the preceding chapters and not all these 'buttons' are key for the right leadership setting.

In order to make it clear, these KLFs are the six main buttons of your mixer and they form the basis of the LiDRS model. They enable you to judge leadership, as well as to think in advance about which features you wish to apply under certain circumstances. Should you wish to have more details, then you can zoom in on the building blocks from the KLFs. By peering at the building blocks, you will automatically influence the six KLFs.

In the next chapter I will further address how the KLFs relate to the LiDRS model and how you can use the model.

10. THE LIDRS MODEL

A tree that wants to grow so fast that it pulls its roots out of the ground, will not float to heaven, but topple over.
-Harry Mulisch- (1927 - 2010)

The core of the LiDRS model is the cluster of building blocks that you were introduced to in the previous chapter. This cluster results in various Key Leadership Features (KLFs) The KLFs are the main buttons that you can turn to adjust the course of your leadership situation. You do not need to look at the building blocks in detail for every situation. The extent to which you deploy or emphasize your KLFs determines how you lead.

You now have several questions to ask yourself about leadership:

1. How do I assess whether or not I am a good leader?

2. In which 'elements of leadership' do I need to develop my skills?

3. How do I assess someone else's leadership features?

4. How do I behave as a leader in extraordinary situations?

By using the LiDRS model, you will be able to answer these and other questions about leadership. The model is a tool to help improve your leadership features, to assess others in terms of leadership and to discover what the effects of leadership are by applying certain building blocks differently.

DIRECTING OR ADJUSTING THE KLFS
The practical use of KLFs generally happens unwittingly, but how often do you find yourself thinking in hindsight, 'I wish I'd done that differently,' or 'Why didn't I think this through a little bit better?' The LiDRS model helps you to determine in advance which features may

be important given the circumstances. How and when you deploy certain KLFs will be influenced by different variables. To understand the variables in a leadership situation, the entire situation is viewed as a black box. You are positioned in this box as a leader and you will deal with three variables: the binding element, the external influence and the people you lead.

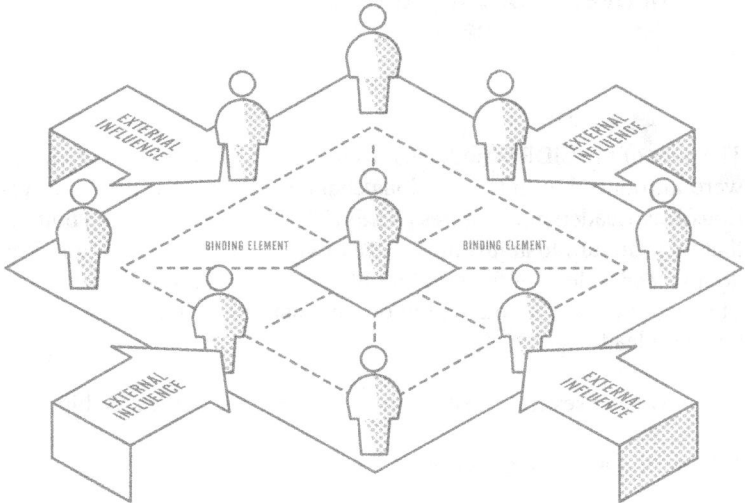

Figure 3: The three leadership variables

The first variable is the **binding element**. This may be an organization or a combined objective. If an organization is the binding element, you may be dealing with different types of organizations. The way you lead will be different in a hierarchical organization as opposed to a flat or network organization. In addition, it is also important to recognize what drives the organization. Is it about knowledge; money or providing a service? If the binding element is a combined objective, it may be something like coaching a sports team or organizing an event.

The second variable that may affect your leadership settings is the **external influences** you are dealing with as a leader. External influence is a broad concept. This has to do with all influences on your leadership. Maybe there is total chaos and uncertainty. Perhaps there is a major reorganization about to start and many fear for their jobs. Or possibly is

172

it just the other way around and everything is running smoothly, without any strain on the system. External influences will cause a certain amount of disturbance for you as a leader. A disturbance may just cause a ripple in the process, or it may turn into a major storm.

The third variable concerns the **persons** you lead and also those from whom you receive directions. What kind of characters and personalities are you dealing with? What is their level of knowledge and experience? For example, if you are dealing with professionals, you will have to assume a different attitude than you would in an organization where people frequently switch positions and require continuous directing and coaching. All of these aspects will result in an adjustment on your part as a leader and will also create a certain pattern of expectations for you as a leader.

THE USE OF THE LIDRS MODEL

The LiDRS model can be used in different ways. The digital model on the website www.lidrs.eu may be of assistance here. Regardless of how you plan to use the LiDRS model, you will first need to answer a few short questions to determine the framework of your specific leadership situation. These questions address the three variables referred to above and will help you evaluate the building blocks for your specific situation. This valuation is a simple score between 0 and 10. A score of '0' means you will not include this building block in the assessment while a score of '10' means that all of your senses are geared towards this. This will result in a certain level of influence of a KLF. The combination of the six KLFs determines your leadership setting. You can use it for a certain situation and you can also use it as a generic assessment of yourself as a leader. The online tool will provide a quick and simple display of your settings. You can find more on this at www.lidrs.eu.

The LiDRS model can be used in many different ways:

1. As an assessment model

The goal of the assessment model is to make you think about the leadership situation that you are in and the manner in which you will be applying the KLFs. The digital model gives a visualization of application of the KLF in question. This is the setting of your mixing console. By using the assessment model, you will think in advance or in retrospect about leadership and the possibilities to direct or to adjust this in your situation. You will judge yourself for important features of leadership and by the settings of the KLFs you can determine whether this is the most logical choice, given your situation. The assessment model serves as a basis for all other applications of the LiDRS model.

1. As a feedback model

Assessing yourself is helpful if you wish to think about your leadership and determine whether or not you are focusing on the right features. An objective assessment, however, can only be given by other people. The feedback model provides the opportunity to check your settings by asking how you are viewed by others. After filling in the assessment model, you will be given an option to also receive objective feedback from one or more respondents. The advantage of multiple respondents is that they can always respond anonymously and they may even reject your request, without you being informed. Using the feedback you receive, you will see the difference between your leadership settings and the way others assess your leadership.

There is also a possibility to assess not yourself, but a specific leader and assess him in the context of your situation. It is interesting to see for which building blocks this leader scores differently and how this affects his entire way of leading, or the use of his KLFs.

3. As a reference model

You can obviously also learn from others by looking at their settings when the same variables are used. This is another reason to fill in the initial reference questions. The assessment models that have been filled in are collected and made available as a reference model. After filling in your scores, you can look at the reference model. A model will then be provided in a chart, with the same variables you filled in, but possibly showing the KLFs at different settings. By learning from the settings of others and in particular by looking at the outcome of these settings, your leadership experience will grow. The result is interesting, of course. Has the person reached his objective? In retrospect, would a different setting have been better?

Quality assessments are important for the interpretation of the model.

174

Here you can find out why the settings of the KLFs were chosen as they were. This way you will not only learn from your own feedback, but also from the choices made by others.

4. As a simulation model

The LiDRS model can also be used to look at the effects of changing the settings of KLFs. For example, what happens in my situation if I put less effort into my guiding features? Adjusting this KLF downwards without looking at the building blocks, will directly influence the other KLFs. Therefore, it appears that these six KLFs are in communication. The use of the LiDRS model as a simulation model provides insight into the consequences of too little or too much influence of the KLFs.

These are all theories of the application of the LiDRS model, of course. Eventually, you will be using the model itself. For optimal use of the LiDRS model, you will need to know how the various KLFs are constituted. In the following paragraphs, I will further address the six Key Leadership Features. All of the definitions of the building blocks are included in Appendix 2 .

KLF 1: SOCIAL FEATURES
What makes a social person? Why is a person good at interacting with others? Which features make people like you? Social features encourage you to think of others. You are able to envision the effects of what you do or say on other people. You are **people-oriented** and show a strong level of **empathy**. Social features are not all about how much other people like you, however. You are also capable of saying things as they are at the right moments and when necessary you can draw attention with a good story. You are able to touch people with your story. This is because you have good **communication skills**. The people are willing to work for and with you, because of the person that you really are. People **trust** you for who you are, for what you do and for how you say things. You are as you are and that makes you **authentic** in all of your actions.

Social features are also where you come across as honestly **interested** and where you prioritize the other person.

Leaders are not always people with the types of social features that enable them to maneuver smoothly in a group. Sometimes the leader is a narcissist. Self-confidence and a high opinion of oneself are useful and perhaps even essential for a leader,[38] but a leader always needs to have social features. This is supported by the definition of leadership from the previous chapter. Applying these features at the right time and being **tactful** will allow you to achieve a support base for your leadership.

Social features are applied differently in every situation. In relatively calm circumstances where there is not too much external pressure and you feel as a leader that you need to assume a more vulnerable attitude, you will need those social features to fall back on.

You apply social features less prominently when the mental distance between the leader and the followers needs to be widened. These are often situations with great external pressure and disappointing results. It is in those times that followers seem to need a leader who will take the reins and sometimes take hard, but particularly firm, action.

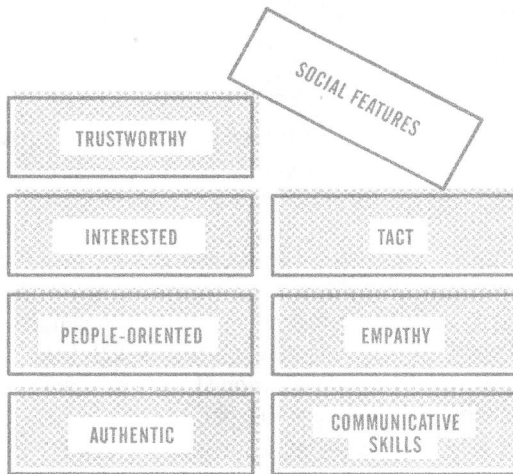

SOCIAL FEATURES

TRUSTWORTHY	
INTERESTED	TACT
PEOPLE-ORIENTED	EMPATHY
AUTHENTIC	COMMUNICATIVE SKILLS

Figure 4: Building blocks of social features

---

[38] T.R. Horton - CEO paradox; The Privilege and Accountability of Leadership; American Management Association, New York, 1992

KLF 2: OBSERVED FEATURES

Based on your observations, you form an opinion. The observed features are where, through your actions, you wittingly or unwittingly influence the observations of others and, inherently, their opinion. Therefore, this concerns the observations of others. You often are not aware of the application of these features and you cannot influence them. Think here of **charisma**, for example. Charisma is an individual quality that distinguishes the man from the 'common' man, causing him to be treated as a leader.[39] However, you have very little control over this particular quality. Others do have opinions about it, however.

You do, however, have an influence on **flair** and image. By displaying your flair at the right moments, you will influence the way in which people observe you. However, there is a pitfall here. Others may observe your well-intended flair as 'stuck-up' or 'arrogant'. Thus, you need to show flair based on a smart and charming image. You can also influence observations by presenting yourself properly, so do this the right way and make sure you look impeccable. Your entire image must be correct. You emanate calm and confidence. You are a leader and therefore you know you must have a **proper appearance**.

A leader has **self-confidence**. In addition to that self-confidence, he must also have confidence in his team, in his people and in his plan. It is also up to the leader to instill that confidence in his people. Confidence in yourself and in your people will make everybody perform better.

People like a leader to emanate **calm**. This doesn't mean that you feel calm or that you actually are calm, you just know what the effects are on others when you emanate calm. You influence their perception.

Stress resistance is a bit more difficult to learn, but it is inextricably linked to the observed features. Individual stress arises when there is a lack of internal room to maneuver. The internal room to maneuver is your ability to consider the options. There are several ways to increase this internal room for maneuver: by knowledge, by experience, but also by sharing your challenges and asking for the opinions of others. By increasing your internal room to maneuver, you reduce the chances of stress. The stress reaction also occurs in groups or organizations when

---

[39] Max Weber on Charisma and institution building; The University of Chicago Press, Chicago, 1968.

the well-being of the group is threatened. This stress may result in poor decisions. Instead of a thorough analysis of the situation based on years of knowledge and experience, people under stress often impulsively turn to unproductive, intuitive reactions that fulfill a direct, personal, emotional need. In a stressful situation, however, an objective assessment from the leader is required. A team will also handle stress better when the leader manages to transform personal worries into attempts to achieve common goals.[40] This is why a leader should prevent a situation where stress gains the upper hand and spreads among the group. The observed features of both yourself and the group will control the stress level.

You should realize that the observed features are about having an awareness of how your actions will affect others. It is therefore necessary to find the right balance between being yourself and laying down a perception or observation at all times, in accordance with the social building block 'authentic'.

```
              ┌─────────────────────────────┐
              │      OBSERVED FEATURES       │
              └─────────────────────────────┘

  ┌─────────────────────┐   ┌─────────────────────┐
  │        CALM         │   │   SELF-CONFIDENCE   │
  └─────────────────────┘   └─────────────────────┘

  ┌─────────────────────┐   ┌─────────────────────┐
  │   STRESS-RESISTANT  │   │      CHARISMA       │
  └─────────────────────┘   └─────────────────────┘

  ┌─────────────────────┐   ┌─────────────────────┐
  │      OBLIGING       │   │        FLAIR        │
  └─────────────────────┘   └─────────────────────┘
```

Figure 5: Building blocks of Observed features

[40] B.M. Bass, R.E. Reggio - Transformational Leadership; Lawrence Erlbaum Associates, New Jersey, 2006

KLF 3: ACTION FEATURES

Many elements play a part in the process of being accepted as a leader. In the end, you will be the leader for what you do and not because you say that you are the leader or find yourself in a leadership position.[41] You can shout from the rooftops that you are the leader but, eventually, you will have to act the part. You set the example for people to follow.

This means that when the situation so demands, you have to be able to put your foot down or to make unpopular decisions. This requires **courage** and sometimes these unpopular decisions may require a leader to assume a **hard** attitude. Courage is what separates the leader from the manager. The leader will regularly be required to display courage by acting **vigorously** and **decisively**. This means you will have to make decisions that may not be universally supported but which will benefit the organization, or ensure the organization achieves its objectives, regardless of how many discussions took place regarding the matter in question. Once a decision has been made, the entire team will support it. Research has shown that, in times of stress, groups and organizations want and expect to receive directive leadership.[42] As a leader in a stressful situation, you will sometimes need to take hard action and often assume the lead with courage, which will lead to support for your leadership.

The leader is critical, both of himself as well as of his people. Why settle for 'average' when it could also be 'excellent?' This **demand** and high **ambition** on the part of a leader and the corresponding pattern of expectation ensures that people will also have high demands and ambitions for themselves. Your people expect you to be critical. As such, they will not settle for an 'average' performance themselves. This is, obviously, not an intrinsic motivation, but triggered by your high demands.

The high pattern of expectation is enhanced by acting **consistent** at all times - consistent in setting high demands, consistent in your method of directing and consistent in your behavior. This consistency will ensure that people know what to expect from you. Nothing is more annoying than a leader whose reaction no one can predict.

---

[41] Y. Couchard - Let My People Go Surfing, The Education of a Reluctant Businessman; Penguin Books, New York, 2006

[42] B.M. Bass - The Bass Handbook of Leadership; Free Press, New York, 2008

179

This causes a lot of uncertainty. It is up to the leader to provide a relatively relaxed working environment where others may excel. The leader must also have an above-average level of **perseverance**. Where others stop, you will distinguish yourself by refusing to give up.

The leader is **proactive**. He does not sit back and wait for solutions to come to him; he goes in search of answers and solutions himself. If people know that their leader is proactive, they will also assume a proactive attitude.

Finally, the leader will need to take **responsibility** for his actions, but also for his team's actions. By taking responsibility, even when things are not going well, you will solidify your leadership role. Man, by nature tends to seek for external causes for failures and bad results. However, the leader takes responsibility and makes sure to learn from his mistakes.

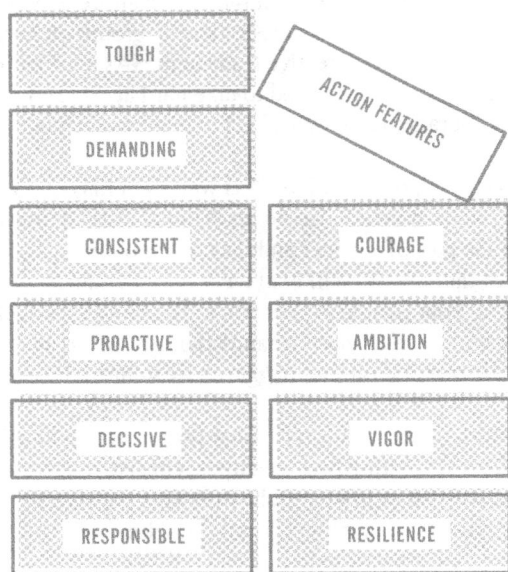

Figure 6: Building blocks of Action features

KLF 4: DIPLOMATIC FEATURES

Your proactive attitude, your hard approach and your vigorous performance will not always generate the best result. You will regularly need to use your diplomatic features. This way you will achieve your goal in a more subtle, well thought-out and circuitous way. Two steps forward, one step back. Your diplomatic features enable you to view everything in a wider perspective. The action features will take you from A to B in the shortest possible time, quickly clearing obstacles. Diplomatic features take a detour around the obstacles, subtly convincing people to cooperate and achieve your goal. You must accept other parties for what they are and prevent both yourself as well as these other parties from losing face at all costs. The diplomatic features support the observed features. After all, by applying diplomatic features, you leave an impression with others. The reason for applying this is not always to influence the perception as in the observed features, but to achieve the final goal.

What are these diplomatic features? First, there is the capacity to **negotiate**. The real tradesman will be able to buy or sell an article at the best price, being satisfied with this and leaving the other party with a good feeling as well. Both parties are satisfied.

You are **articulate** both orally and in writing and you know how to apply the right regulations at the right time. **Etiquette** is something with which you were raised. Whatever you do, people will be able to take you as an **example** or as a role model. Setting the example increasingly becomes the rule of thumb in the business world these days, more and more emphasized in the policies of big enterprises. **Integrity** is closely connected to this. Are you able to look at yourself in the mirror? At times when you get the gut feeling that something is amiss, what decision will you make? Again, you are not who you say you are, you are what you do.

Finally, the diplomat is able to assess certain customs and cultures for what they are actually worth. This **cultural awareness** enables you to emanate the same perception anywhere in the world, under any circumstances.

Diplomatic features are blended into the system of a leader. Therefore, your diplomatic features inherently play a role in all situations. There are situations however, where you lay emphasis on these features: a first meeting, attracting a new customer, getting the group to cooperate;

these are just a few examples. With your diplomatic features, you can distinguish yourself from other people in leadership positions.

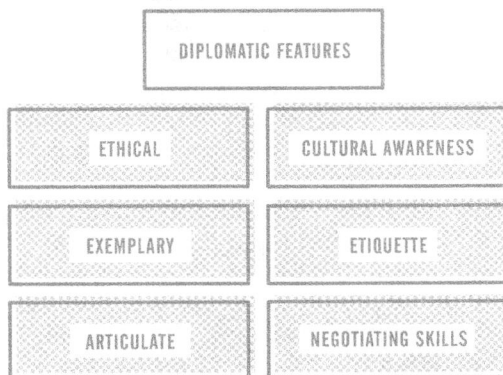

Figure 7: Building blocks of Diplomatic features

KLF 5: MENTAL FEATURES

How important are mental features? Can the leader suffice with a healthy dose of charisma and the ability to take action every now and then? Maybe add a few social skills and then you have a leader? It appears that more is required to be able to practice good leadership at all levels. In addition to all of the features just mentioned, the leader will also need to use his brains effectively.

The leader with **know-how** will have a certain degree of authority over others, which makes accepting his leadership easier. That does not mean, however, that a person without much know-how can't achieve authority within a group of people. By asking the right questions, for example and applying your analytical capacities, this can be done. **Analytical capacity** enables you to distinguish main points from minor points and to find creative solutions. In this way, you are able to set priorities. As a leader, you must think ahead and your **creativity** helps you to think about all possible scenarios. What will be my next step and how might this play out? Although you have little influence on your analytical capacity and creativity, these elements are proof of a certain form of

182

intelligence. Obviously, **intelligence** is also linked to the speed of basic information processing and the capacity of your working memory. In short, he who is intelligent can think fast and take multiple issues into account.[43] However, as we saw earlier, the differences between people are marginal. Other forms of intelligence, like social and emotional intelligence, are incorporated into other KLFs.

The leader has an above-average level of **curiosity**. Everybody who works with and for you is aware of this. If you are inquisitive, you will ask questions, showing that you are actually interested in the work of your staff. This curiosity ensures that you want answers about issues that are unclear.

Your mental features also ensure that you have **self-knowledge** and that you are a good **judge of character**. You know exactly what your strengths and weaknesses are and more importantly, you know how to handle them. You know when to listen to your 'gut feeling', your intuition. You also know how to get the best out of others. The leader knows his people and knows their strengths, but also their weaknesses.

The leader has vision. A vision that reaches further than tomorrow. Vision means to have foresight, a view towards the future. Where do I want the organization to go? A vision directs your people in the big picture. Having vision also means that you can think about the strategic implications of your actions in the long term. A leader with vision makes decisions by thoroughly weighing the pros and cons and the consequences for the future. A vision provides coherence and direction in the tasks and actions we undertake.

Besides this, the leader is also a person with **situational awareness**. He cannot be coerced into being absorbed by one single problem, but he will maintain oversight of the big picture. He is aware of the fact that stress may impede objective thought. By using a helicopter view at the right moments, he will ask himself, 'What does this really mean?' This seemingly simple question is easily forgotten when you are absorbed in a process or a problem. Every leader should regularly ask himself the '*So what?*' and '*What does this mean?*'

---

[43] Asendorpf - *Psychologie van de persoonlijkheid* - about personality psychology; Springer Medizin Verlag, Heidelberg, 2009

Apart from the fact that the leader maintains an overview, he must also be able to **put matters into perspective**. A lack of this capability actually means that your situational awareness is gone. You are sucked into a problem and no longer see this in the big picture; the situation looks a lot different.

Finally, **discipline** will support your ability to distinguish yourself in mental features. You are disciplined in the way that you work, but also in your actions. Discipline ensures that you look your best every day, but also that you arrive at work on time and that you keep your appointments. Discipline requires a certain level of dedication to undertake certain actions and stimulation of the mind. Discipline ensures that you get out of bed in the morning to be at work on time and prevents you from being lured by pleasures when they interfere with your work. Discipline empowers your sense of duty and this is what is expected of any leader.

Mental features are difficult to influence. You can't suddenly think, 'Today I will be intelligent, creative or extra curious.' However, there are definitely ways to influence this KLF.

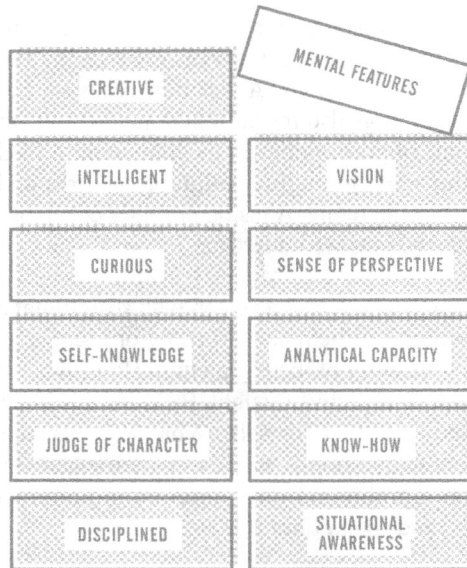

CREATIVE	MENTAL FEATURES
INTELLIGENT	VISION
CURIOUS	SENSE OF PERSPECTIVE
SELF-KNOWLEDGE	ANALYTICAL CAPACITY
JUDGE OF CHARACTER	KNOW-HOW
DISCIPLINED	SITUATIONAL AWARENESS

Figure 8: Building blocks of mental features

KLF 6: GUIDING FEATURES

The leader has the capacity to direct matters according to his wishes. A name for this, which may be interpreted negatively, is influence, but what you eventually wish to achieve as leader is to steer certain processes. You want to get the best out of your team and out of the process. One of the tools of the leader is to assume a **coaching role**. The leader is able to lift his people to a higher level. The coach adjusts, asks the right questions, gives compliments as appropriate and allows people to excel. In this way, an individual contributes to the process.

This makes the leader a **team builder** as well. He knows how to bind people, to deploy the right features and to push the team to better performances. The leader can influence the morale of the team by the way he leads. He inspires, motivates, and gets people to follow him because of his passion. An inspirational leader knows exactly which buttons to push in people. Because of his inspiration, people are willing to go the extra mile, to deliver a contribution to the group process and to simply follow the leader. Moreover, an inspirational leader reduces feelings of burn-out and stress, as is reported in a study printed in the European Journal of Work and Psychology. Therefore, as a leader, you must have **inspirational** features if you want to get the best out of your team.[44]

The leader can assume an **adaptive** attitude. If the environment changes, the leader will be able to adapt his plans and ideas accordingly. The leader is **competitive** by nature. Participating will not suffice, winning is the creed. Second place means you are the first to lose. It is this competitive attitude and the refusal to settle for 'average' that ensure your drive to grow and improve. Here, your social features will ensure that you do not become an obnoxious person with whom no one wants to work. It is clear that demanding and competitive are closely connected. The trick is to find a balance where you are competitive, while not losing sight of your social features.

Directing also means that the leader knows how to **delegate** tasks to the right people at the right time. After all, this supports his mental ability to maintain oversight of the situation. In order to be able to delegate properly, you must be able to **organize**.

---

[44] European Journal of Work and Psychology, Volume 8, March 1999, Psychology Press ltd., East Sussex, UK

Who will take on which tasks, when will I complete certain processes, do the deadlines link up with each other? Delegating and organizing are not linked to 'directing' for nothing.

Finally 'directing' means that you are able to convince people of your opinions. You are the inspirational leader. You are able to convince people of the fact that you are right, based on the arguments, but also based on your attitude, flair and belief. People want to follow you and believe in the direction you choose.

```
                    ┌─────────────────────┐
                    │   GUIDING FEATURES   │
                    └─────────────────────┘

  ┌─────────────────────┐   ┌─────────────────────┐
  │      ADAPTIVE        │   │   PERSUASIVENESS     │
  └─────────────────────┘   └─────────────────────┘

  ┌─────────────────────┐   ┌─────────────────────┐
  │     COMPETITIVE      │   │   COACHING SKILLS    │
  └─────────────────────┘   └─────────────────────┘

  ┌─────────────────────┐   ┌─────────────────────┐
  │    INSPIRATIONAL     │   │  ABILITY TO DELEGATE │
  └─────────────────────┘   └─────────────────────┘

  ┌─────────────────────┐   ┌─────────────────────┐
  │    TEAM BUILDER      │   │   ORGANIZATIONAL     │
  │                      │   │      CAPACITY        │
  └─────────────────────┘   └─────────────────────┘
```

Figure 9: Building blocks of guiding features

The descriptions above explain all the buttons of your individual mixer. You will mainly use KLFs, but when you really go further into it, you will look at all building blocks and take the time to carefully study your own situation and personal settings.

PRACTICE MAKES PERFECT
The building blocks give the leader more insight in the meaning of the KLFs. It is obviously impossible to ask yourself which building block to apply for everything you do, how you can direct and whether you are doing a good job.

It is important that you are able to switch between the different KLFs. In general, this is a natural process. All features and building blocks are present at all times, but you don't always have to apply them all, that would be far too complex. A lot of this also depends on your gut feeling or intuition. Experience will help to assess situations quickly and to see which building block would be best to use. This is why experience is an important advantage you have as a leader. But also without experience, you will be able to work with the LiDRS model, as long as you are aware of the different options and the buttons you can turn. Follow your intuition, evaluate your actions regularly and look at others and how they use their building blocks.

Whether you are experienced or a beginner, you can always think about the six KLFs. In every situation, these six features flash through your mind. What is expected of me, do I lay emphasis on my social features or is it time for action? Do I issue the right signals that enhance the perception? The message you wish to convey must be in harmony with the extent to which you apply your KLFs. The actual fine-tuning of your 'mixer' can always follow later.

THE LIDRS MODEL IN USE
Now you have the building blocks, the KLFs and you know the model can be used in various ways online. But what does the LiDRS model really look like?

First, there is the 'building blocks LiDRS model' (Figure 10). This is just a cluster of the building blocks you saw earlier. In the online version, you can add scores to the building blocks in this model. The LiDRS model itself is an interplay between KLFs. By attaching a value to your building blocks, the result will affect the KLFs. The LiDRS model works like the synthesizer on your stereo. In Figure 11, you see that Hans has awarded higher grades to himself on the building blocks of the guiding features and lower grades on the building blocks of the action features. What is interesting, subsequently, is the interplay between the KLFs. Hans immediately spots where his focus lies and he can assess whether this is the right focus for his situation. The intensity with which you apply a KLF is displayed by the height of the chart.

Knowledge, experience, character and personality are important features in a leader. The more baggage you have, the firmer the model will stand. Quickly applying KLFs or switching between the KLFs will be done intuitively as you become more experienced as a leader. You are working on it, but it does not require long preparations or evaluations.

If you are using the feedback feature of the online model, you will not only see all the settings of the LiDRS model, but you will also see the presentation of an overlay displaying how others have assessed you. This is a means by which to compare your perception of leadership with observations from others.

The standard of the LiDRS model is flexible. Visualizing which KLF has your emphasis is essential. The leader who has developed himself in all aspects of leadership may score high points on all fronts at the same time. Perhaps there is a lower limit of 8 or 9, but then the chart

Figure 10:
The building
blocks of the
LiDRS model

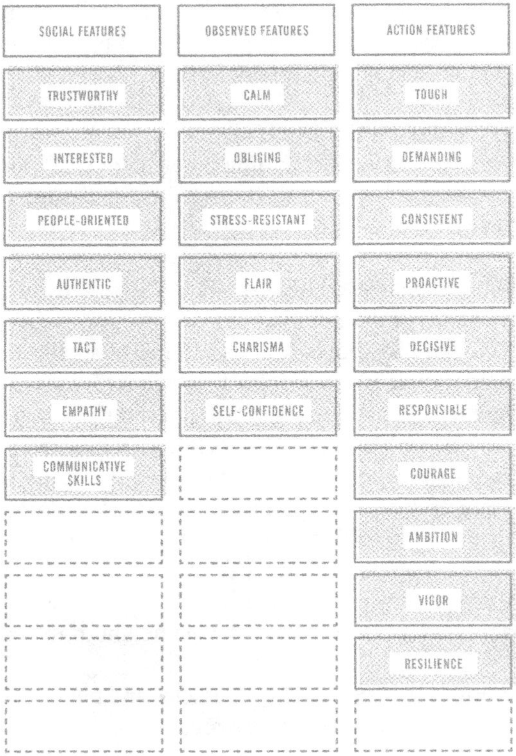

SOCIAL FEATURES	OBSERVED FEATURES	ACTION FEATURES
TRUSTWORTHY	CALM	TOUGH
INTERESTED	OBLIGING	DEMANDING
PEOPLE-ORIENTED	STRESS-RESISTANT	CONSISTENT
AUTHENTIC	FLAIR	PROACTIVE
TACT	CHARISMA	DECISIVE
EMPATHY	SELF-CONFIDENCE	RESPONSIBLE
COMMUNICATIVE SKILLS		COURAGE
		AMBITION
		VIGOR
		RESILIENCE

will still have a similar structure. It is about the application of the right KLFs in their mutual coherence. The coherence of the features indicates how you apply your leadership features based in the variables referred to earlier. Obviously, an experienced leader may also ask himself question whether or not too much emphasis on all KLFs is the right approach ....

With the LiDRS model, you can assess the way your mixer is tuned by simply using the variables and assessing the building blocks you wish to apply. Simply adding value to building blocks does not improve the outcome of the model, as this is also about an assessment of quality. If you are using a reference model after filling in your model, one that somebody else has already filled in with the same variables, the qualitative information is precisely what is important. Why have the settings been chosen as they have and has it generated the desired effect?

DIPLOMATIC FEATURES	MENTAL FEATURES	GUIDING FEATURES
ETHICAL	CREATIVE	ADAPTIVE
EXEMPLARY	INTELLIGENT	COMPETITIVE
ARTICULATE	CURIOUS	INSPIRATIONAL
ETIQUETTE	SELF-KNOWLEDGE	TEAM BUILDER
CULTURAL AWARENESS	JUDGE OF CHARACTER	PERSUASIVENESS
NEGOTIATING SKILLS	DISCIPLINED	COACHING SKILLS
	VISION	ABILITY TO DELEGATE
	SENSE OF PERSPECTIVE	ORGANIZATIONAL CAPACITY
	ANALYTICAL CAPACITY	
	KNOW-HOW	
	SITUATIONAL AWARENESS	

GROWING AS A LEADER

Eventually, you want to grow as a leader. You are not a leader just for the fun of it and you have certain features that are a driving force for further growth. Growth as a leader can be measured in several ways. There are likely certain hierarchical steps you can take. Growth may also be linked to the budget you have at your disposal or the number of people you direct. In general, there is a relationship between the level of leadership and your degree of responsibility. As the level of leadership changes, the KLFs will need to be updated. If you gain additional responsibilities, you will also apply your KLFs differently. These KLFs develop through growth in knowledge, experience, personality and character.

You can influence the building blocks by expanding your knowledge. You can make yourself an expert in all sorts of fields and you can determine for yourself when to apply this knowledge. Growth in experience

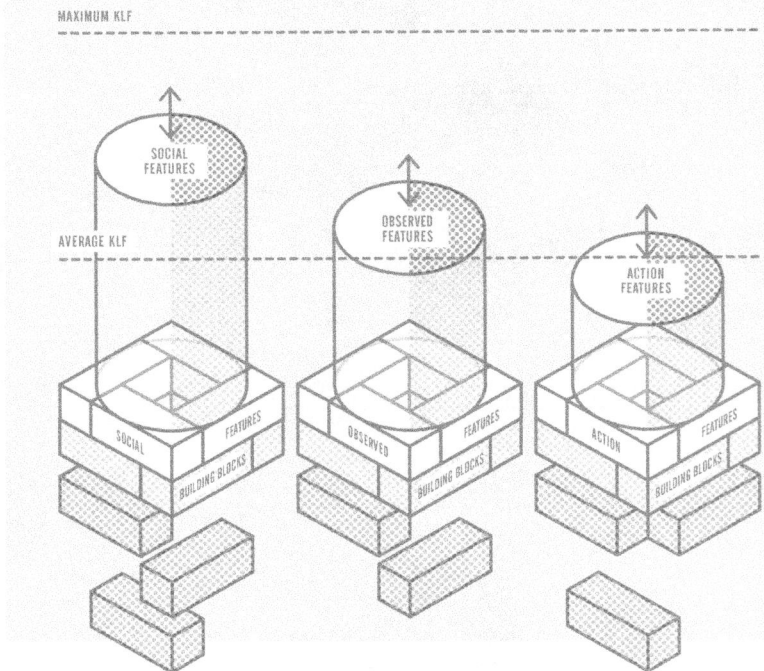

Figure 11: The LiDRS model filled in by Hans

will require a bit more patience. You gain experience by taking steps yourself and by involvement in events, but also by looking at others. Ask yourself regularly, 'What would I have done in this situation?' or 'What do I think of how he handled this?' Character and personality are a bit more difficult to influence. After all, character and personality, or that which sets us apart from others, are inherent qualities. A fair share of KLFs are closely connected to character and personality features. Think of resilience, mental resistance and vigor, being people-oriented and demanding. Indeed, we get these features at an early age, but in later life is when you will be able to put things into perspective and value things for what they are really worth.

Of course, there are people who are born winners. If participating is more important to you than winning, however, and you are aware of this, then it is time for you to take steps towards leadership.

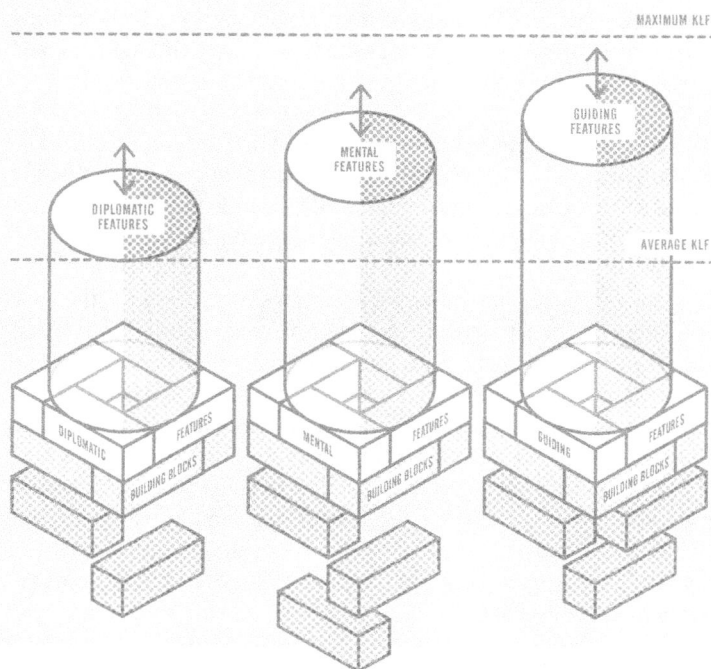

Adapting personality and character is hard, but pushing yourself to display leadership behavior, which may not be in your nature, is where the challenge lies. Participating is no longer enough, you want to win! You are the one to determine when to coach or when to bang your fist on the table. This is the moment when you are aware of the impression you wish to leave behind and of the attitude that you will need to assume to achieve this.

WHICH STEPS DO YOU MAKE IN LEADERSHIP?

The question is which strategy you will use to move forward as a leader. You can obviously wait and see what opportunities come along; however, I believe that it is be better to take matters into your own hands. The LiDRS model can help you with this. Suppose you want to have a higher position. You wonder which building blocks you need to be able to function as a leader on that higher level. Look at the specific job or position in the organization and check for yourself which building blocks are the most important. How do you score on these building blocks? For which building blocks must you intentionally train? Which building blocks are difficult to influence and which are easy? You are expected to assess yourself objectively to receive the most accurate results.

Then you go work on these building blocks. All of your actions will be focused on leadership on a higher level. The advantage of this is that the actual steps are not as large and it is all related to perception. Others will also see you as the appropriate leader for a higher position.

If you have doubts about assessing the settings of your KLFs, then ask yourself the why-question with every assessment. You will often find out too late where things went wrong. The errors will slowly creep up in your actions, triggered by high job pressure or perhaps because you are blind to your own mistakes. By taking the time to look critically at your settings, you will reduce the blindness and limit management on an ad hoc basis. How much time does it cost to sit back and objectively evaluate your settings? Is my evaluation of the binding elements, external influences and persons still correct? Considering these variables, are my KLFs set correctly? Simple questions, but essential questions if you want to grow as a leader.

STAY CLOSE TO YOURSELF

Of course, there are leaders who will score poorly on their KLFs if they ask for feedback. There are leaders who openly have doubts about everything, who have a chronic lack of charisma and will go to work in an old pair of blue jeans. However, if these people are running a company worth billions or have built their own empire, then this is truly unique leadership. Unfortunately, this is not for everyone. If you believe that you are such a leader and you can afford to show this, good luck! Many have tried before you, but only a few have actually become leaders. According to the American consultancy agency Towers Perrin, European managers are not team players; they are not enterprising enough and not very innovative. The low quality of leadership is due to the mediocre potential of leaders. Ten percent are natural talents, thirty percent should never have become a leader and sixty percent have to work hard to make something of it.[45] Others justify your leadership. It seems to me a safer option to work within the 'standard' frames of the optimal application of your KLFs and justify your leadership through this.

What you can and must do is distinguish yourself through authenticity. This means staying close to yourself and acting open, honest and sincere. The leadership role you assume must not be just an act, but a real way of leading about which you also feel good. The closer you are to yourself, the easier it is to lead. It will cost you less energy, it will be easier for you to improve your leadership features and you will justify your leadership sooner. In short, no matter how you apply the LiDRS model, you will always need to stay close to yourself in order to get the maximum out of it.

TO REMEMBER
The LiDRS model helps you to think about your leadership style in a specific situation. It directs your thoughts and is also a guideline for feedback. You can quickly run through the LiDRS model by only looking at the KLFs, but if you take more time to do a thorough evaluation afterwards or a well thought-out estimation in advance, then the LiDRS model can help you. Finally, there are the pre-filled models, which, based on lessons learned, will considerably expand your leadership frame of reference. In the end, you will need to implement the model in all of its applications and you will see that all these tools will help you to grow as a leader.

---

[45] J.D. den Breejen – *De high performance Organisatie; Een integrale aanpak; Management van leren en veranderen*; Kluwer, Alphen aan de Rijn, 2009

11. THE LEADER OF THE FUTURE

Never let the future disturb you. You will meet it, if you have to, with the same weapons of reason which today arm you against the present
-Marcus Aurelius- (121 - 180)

The world around us is changing fast. Organizations do their best to be frontrunners and trendsetters. Their leaders are also expected to be frontrunners. The leader needs to assume an adaptive attitude, move along with the market and with the environment, catering to changing wishes of customers, but also of the staff and the world, as they perceive it. Along with these changing circumstances, there also are universal features of leadership. Features that are still necessary for a leader, in spite of a changing environment. In this chapter, I will address the dynamic, changing features that may influence leadership in the near and distant future. I will start with the dynamics of a changing environment. I am referring specifically to directing on output, networks, growing access to information, rising levels of educational and, finally, to managing up.

DIRECTING ON OUTPUT
Employees are increasingly able to work the hours they want from the location that is the most convenient for them. The movement of '*Alternative workplace strategies*' seeks a balance between the type of work, often knowledge-intensive, and the type of worker, often highly educated, so that there is plenty of room for creativity and innovation.[46]

All these developments have consequences for the manner of leading. Maybe in the past you have enjoyed directing the process of your staff, but now you will need to have more faith and you can often only direct on output. After all, your staff have no incentives anymore, no need to sit in bumper-to-bumper traffic on Monday morning in order to be at the weekly meeting at half past eight.

---

[46] R. Baane, P. Houtkamp, M. Knotter – *Het nieuwe werken ontrafeld: Over Bricks Bytes & Behavior* – about unravelling alternative workplace strategies; Koninklijke van Gorcum, Assen, 2011

As a leader, your observed features are secondary if you have little to no contact with your staff. It is great to have all these charismatic leadership features, but at home, behind your laptop, logged in by your VPN, there are only a few people who will notice these features. The trick for this type of leader is to build a team, get people to follow your vision and to find the right settings with which to reach your people.

NETWORKING

Organizations and their market are becoming larger all the time. Globalization is key. Why would you limit your market to prospects within easy driving distance, if just a little effort puts the whole world within your grasp? Globalization, however, creates quite a snap for the leader. It no longer matters what you know, but instead who you know. This cliché applies more so now than ever. You can hardly distinguish yourself by knowledge alone with in today's labor market. You can distinguish yourself by who you know, however. Through various social media platforms, you can easily find out whom you know in the field you are pursuing.

The world is shrinking and networking plays an intricate part in this. Your mental quality remains necessary of course, but if you do not know for sure, there is always someone in your network who does and who will be able to help you. As a leader, you are therefore also expected to be able to work together in a network organization, to know how to assemble the right people around you with the relevant networks. What is worth more for a leader: an employee with the most up to date education in a specific field, or the employee with over a thousand acquaintances in the field? This shift also impacts the application of your KLFs. Particularly important in network organizations is the people you know and who knows you. Clearly this means that the demands on your diplomatic and social features are much stronger.

COLLECTING INFORMATION

The amount of information that a manager needs to process has grown considerably over the past years. Just look at the new information you are bombarded with on a daily basis. Advertisements, e-mails and the amount of information on television, but also meetings, teleconferences and other forms of consultation. The human absorption capacity has become a bottleneck, largely due to the speed at which this information is generated. Somehow, we must find a way to determine how much and which information we need to retain. Take a look at the emails you get in one day, both business and personal correspondence, and see how much of this information you actually need. Check out how many attachments you receive. How many documents have you saved, knowing full well that you will never look at them again? How often are you included in CCs or BCCs of e-mail messages, without the topic being of any concern to you?

This overflow of information will need to be curtailed somehow. In the future, we will need to find proactive solutions to information management. Instead of information being *pushed* at us, we will seek out information from the source. Social networks are an excellent example of a medium that works like this. Instead of getting information sent to us directly, we determine which information we need. Your network posts information and you determine what to read and from whom. In essence, you collect information yourself.

Organizations will work more and more with this *pull* method. Already, projects that are run by a project group are using the network principle, pushing and pulling information. The leaders themselves then determine which information they gather on their own and for which information they wish to receive a notification. The influence this development has on your KLF is in the area of mental features. It speaks to the speed with which you are able to process information with and your ability to determine for yourself which information you must pull or have pushed.

DIRECTING THE HIGHER EDUCATED

The number of graduates with professional and university degrees has increased enormously in the last generations. Besides this, the new generation of graduates is enterprising and internationally oriented. They are the products of a society based on easy access to information and they have developed their own way of processing this information.

This means that the features expected of a leader in a knowledge organization, where you direct twenty university graduates who mainly perform operational work, have changed. As your career progresses, it seems logical that you will be in the knowledge environment, rather than in the production environment. Arguments like 'We will do it this way, because I say so and because we always do it this way' will cause arguments, as your highly educated staff will want to have a say,

197

adjust ideas and make decisions. Not only are you expected to have the necessary mental features, but also the action features to distinguish yourself from the group.

Indeed, people must think along with you and we need to stimulate this, but we should specifically guard against merely talking and not making decisions. It is up to you to encourage everyone think along, but eventually only one person is responsible for making a decision and that is you!

MANAGING UP

The number of leaders and their level of responsibility have increased due to the cost reduction efforts and the goal of maximum efficiency within large and global organizations. There is a good possibility, therefore, that within an organization, you both provide and receive leadership. There also is a greater chance that someone with the wrong settings on his KLFs will be directing you. Since you are the potential leader, you will be expected to be able to direct upward in the right way. This managing-up is often one of the biggest challenges for new leaders. How many potential leaders have become stranded in their current position by one obstacle or one collision of characters?

In order to deal with this, a lot is expected of your diplomatic features. The trick is to acquire a support base for your work, but also for your personal competences. Your leader will feel threatened if you take away all his sense of himself as 'leader'.

Your challenge is to eliminate his concerns. You are not a threat to him. You are his solution. Slowly but surely, you create a bond with a leader, you keep him in his seat, but at the right moments, you openly make it clear to him that there is no way around your competences. In the conversations you have, you know your own role and place and you respect his leading role and emphasize that neither of you needs to lose face.[47] You appeal to your diplomatic, observed and guiding features.

---

[47] S. Gerritsen - *Een goed gesprek, Over communicatieve vaardigheden* – about communicative skills; Uitgeverij Nieuwezijds, Amsterdam, 2001

STABILITY IN A CHANGING ENVIRONMENT

Certain building blocks of the KLF remain unchanged. It does not matter in which situation you are yourself, which people you lead or what the organization you work for looks like. They are the building blocks you not necessarily use as a leader, but as a person. Examples of these unchanged building blocks of leadership are integrity, charisma and your empathetic ability. They are the constant high scores in the LiDRS model.

There will always be a need for leaders, a need for people whose example we would like to follow, for people who look after our interests. Leaders are necessary for processes to run effectively and efficiently. The leader thinks of long-term strategies and eventually he is someone who manages to turn a number of individuals into a team. Based on the dynamics of a changing environment, it can be deduced that a leader will have a challenge on his hands where it concerns applying his features. However, he can reassure himself that his competences are still very much required.

People wish to be taken seriously, they need to be listened to, and many consider themselves leaders, especially when all goes well and there is credit to be earned. That is, right until the moment when things go wrong, then suddenly all eyes are on you. You were the leader, were you not? This is what happens when leadership structures are not entirely clear and the search for a 'scapegoat' is on. Suddenly, nobody is a leader anymore and we are all experts at burying our heads in the sand. We twist and turn in such a way that we disappear behind the broad backs of others.

When the results disappoint, when there is a crisis, this is when the leaders rise up: the people willing to take responsibility. Yes indeed, I am in charge here! You make yourself a bit wider, so others will have more room behind you. These are the moments when you distinguish yourself. Your action features and observed features are put to the test and you must apply them here. This is the moment and you can sense it. Perhaps you would have preferred to rise as leader at another time. At a time when all is well and the team feels that they have put in an especially great performance. However, moments like this, when everybody wants to duck for cover, are the moments when perception starts to come alive. The perception of your team. You rise and justify your leadership. All that you have to do is apply the proper KLFs and the moment is presented to you gift-wrapped. Everybody knows how the cards have been dealt. You are the leader. You knew it long before, of course.

BAD DECISION

The leader makes decisions in a changing world as well. It is necessary and it is expected of him. The justification of the leader is in serious jeopardy if he cannot make a decision. In this case, it is better a poor decision than no decision at all. There will be plenty of examples to show that not deciding worked out well, but if you look at the justification of your leadership, it is best if you do make a decision. This way, you anchor your action features. After that, you must use your observed features and social features to determine how to handle the situation. You can adapt your decision, change it or even have it annulled, but anything is better than sitting around wondering, doing nothing and hoping the problem will work itself out. People are looking at you. They expect you to make a decision! That is their perception.

In order to maintain justification of your leadership, you will need to be out ahead of this stage. After all, you can also make decisions based on mental features. You are not a leader just for the heck of it! You can sense that something is expected of your action features. Your brain will be working feverishly; you get information from your team, weigh the pros and cons and make a decision. Everybody knows where they stand; everybody is ready to move on. You may still doubt your decision, but you do not reveal that. From now on, it is all about perception and for this perception in particular, you have made great strides with the decision you just made.

THE RIGHT PERSON IN THE RIGHT PLACE

Everybody needs to grow into a new role. You cannot, with a college degree and a couple of years' experience, all of a sudden run a listed company with 25,000 employees. You grow by falling down and getting back up again. It is often better to take a small tumble in the beginning, then it is to come crashing down from way up the ladder after you've been climbing it for a couple of years.

Leaders need to grow in a process, which is why as a leader you will continuously be assessed for the way you act on a certain level. How do you act when the stress level rises, when people demand more from

200

you, when time is short or the dilemmas become more complex? As a growing leader, these may be small manageable steps. You need to take the time to process your experiences. What have I learned and how will I approach this next time? If these steps become too large and you have no experience to fall back on, then it will become difficult.

However, if you suffer a setback, don't worry about it! Even born leaders, world leaders, have to grow into their role. These leaders, the ones we want to follow, whom have justified their leadership, have all experienced this. They also have the features that are not learned. Fortunately, we can take solace in the fact that there are but a few leaders of this level walking the earth. And generally they use learned skills that both you and I are perfectly capable of learning as well.

Now you can direct on leadership. You know the six buttons you can turn to justify your leadership. In addition to this, you have been given the means by which to go deeper into the KLFs. You know how to study which building blocks are relevant for your situation and learn how to improve yourself. You also know that some building blocks are easier to influence than others.

The online LiDRS model will, in any case, be able to help clarify where you stand as a leader. You learn this out by filling in the assessment model for yourself, asking for feedback from others or by looking at a reference model from someone in a similar situation. It does not matter; you are now on the right track to grow as a leader.

12. REFLECTION

So what is it that makes a leader into a leader? Why does the one leader have the ability to get people to follow while the other does not? With the help of the LiDRS model, you can now answer these questions and point out the right features.

LEADERS AND MANAGERS

There are many who have a great deal of competences but who will never lead. The number of managers nowadays is staggering. Everybody is a manager of something. Back in the day, we had simple organizational structures and it was clear what you did and what your position was. You were an agent, cleaner or manager. These days we have account managers, facilities managers and plant managers. Have we all suddenly become leaders? Clearly the answer is *no*.

Indeed, everybody is a manager. We all manage something or other at work or in our private lives. You could manage the household accounts or your social life or a project worth millions. Leading, on the other hand, is something entirely different. The leader makes decisions, has long-term vision and the ability to create a team. His leadership was justified by others. The manager doesn't need this. After all, he manages. He ensures that everything runs smoothly without too much trouble. The leader, on the other hand, wants to wake up the neighbors, if possible. The manager nods 'yes', the leader asks 'why?' The manager ducks when things go wrong, the leader rises up!

LEARN FROM MISTAKES

As the author of this book, do I know it all? Am I the perfect leader? The answer is: *Most certainly not*! I am constantly asking myself if, in the current situation, I have found the proper leadership settings of my KLFs. During my disappointing experiences and more often afterwards, I discover that I still have not found the right settings of my KLFs. I was lacing the tools to maintain proper control over the situation.

In addition, understanding that a leader can rise and must direct, has influenced my leadership a great deal. You can influence persons and processes in such a way that a support base is created for you as a person and for your work.

YOU ARE A LEADER!

Wherever you work, whichever level you move around on, you will always encounter dilemmas from which you will need to take a step back. Count to ten and assess yourself based on the LiDRS model. Successful leadership lies largely in your own hands. Be critical of yourself and critical of your actions. Make the most of it and do not impose any limits on yourself, others will do that for you. Test yourself, challenge yourself and use the LiDRS model in a practical setting. Ask yourself regularly what your scores are on the Key Leadership Features and how you can justify your leadership. The more you perform beyond your abilities, the more energy it will cost to acquire legitimacy of leadership. This is why it is best to stay close to yourself, knowing who you are and what your limitations are. Should you feel empowered to continue taking strides, by all means, take those strides. You are full of ambition. You are a leader for a reason...

A WORD OF THANKS

Writing a book takes a great deal of blood, sweat and tears, but also a great deal of time. And time is what I am often so short of, as I have no doubt you, readers, are as well. Still, after years of brainstorming, studying people, reading books and lots of discussions, I am able to present the tangible result of my efforts. This could never have been achieved without tremendous support of family, friends, acquaintances and colleagues.

It is impossible to thank everybody separately. I would however like to express my thanks to Monique and my three beautiful sons. First and foremost, without Monique I never could have written this book. She is the one on who I can always rely on for support. She is the one who manages and leads our family life and gives me the opportunity to chase many of my ideas.

You are the best!

APPENDIX 1 REFERENCES

J. Aidar – Develop your leadership skills; Kogan Page, London 2011

H.C. Altmann – *Overtuigen; een kunst die je kunt leren*; about convincing and how to learn it; MVG-verlag, Landsberg am Lech, Germany

Prof. Dr. J.B. Asendorpf – *Psychologie van de persoonlijkheid*; about personality psychology; Springer media, Heidelberg, Germany 2009

R. Baane, P. Houtkamp, M. Knotter - *Het nieuwe werken ontrafeld; over Bricks, Bytes & Behavior*; alternative workplace strategies unraveled; Koninklijke van Gorcum, Assen, 2011

B. M. Bass, R.E. Riggio - Transformational leadership; Lawrence Erlbaum Associates, New Jersey, 2006

B.M. Bass - The Bass Handbook of Leadership; Free Press, New York, 2008

A.H. Bell; D.M. Smith – Learning Team Skills; Pearson Education 2003

J. Bersin – How do leadership strengths vary around the globe? – article 1, November 2012

Drs. J.D. den Breejen - *De high performance organisatie; Een integrale aanpak; Management van leren en veranderen*; Kluwer, Alpen aan de Rijn, 2009

L. Cauffman – *Oplossingsgericht management & coaching; simpel werkt het best*; about solution-oriented management and coaching - keeping it simple works best; Uitgeverij Lemma, Utrecht, 2005

Y. Couchard - Let my people go surfing; the education of a reluctant businessman; Penguin books, New York, 2006

S.R. Covey – *De 7 eigenschappen van effectief leiderschap* - translation of The 7 habits of highly effective people; Uitgeverij Business Contact, Amsterdam, 2007

Drs. S. Dalenberg, Prof. Dr. A.L.W. Vogelaar – *Leiderschapsvisie: theorie en praktijk; Een beschouwing van de visies op leiderschap binnen Defensie* –analysis of visions on leadership Defense department; *Militaire Spectator* – military scientific magazine for the Dutch armed forces; volume 181, nr 5, 2012

R. van Dithuyzen – *Hoe hoort het eigenlijk?;* about etiquette and rules of behaviour; Becht, Haarlem, 2002

M.S. Dobson, D. Singer Dobson – Managing up; 59 ways to build a career-advancing relationship with your boss, AMACOM, New York, 2000

Prof. Dr. R. H. Flören, S.F. Jansen RA – *Management ondernemerschap – De stille kracht van het familiebedrijf* – about the silent power of the family business, Wolters Kluwer, Deventer, 2010

S. Gerritsen – *Een goed gesprek; over communicatieve vaardigheden;* about communicative skills; Nieuwezijds, Amsterdam, 2001

P. Hersey – *Situationeel leiding geven* – A practical model to flexibly respond to changing circumstances; Business Contact, Amsterdam, 2008

G. Hofstede, G.J. Hofstede – *Allemaal andersdenkenden*; about cultural differences; Business Contact, Amsterdam 2005

T.R. Horton - CEO paradox; The privilege and accountability of leadership; American Management Association, New York, 1992

T. IJzermans; L. Eckhardt – *Het woord is nu aan u!; onstpannen spreken in het openbaar*; about relaxed speaking in public, Thema publishing company; 2009

R. de Jongh; *Wat doet stress met ons lichaam en brein?* – article about what stress does to our body and brain – Psychologie magazine, May 2010

M.F.R. Kets – *Wat leiders drijft; een klinische benadering van gedragsverandering in organisaties*; about what drives leaders – a clinical approach to behavioural change in organisations; Uitgeverij Nieuwezijds, Amsterdam, 2007

J. Kotter, H. Rathgeber – *Onze ijsberg smelt - succesvol veranderen in moeilijke omstandigheden*; about successful changes under difficult circumstances Business Contact, Amsterdam, Antwerp, 2008

M. Maccoby – Narcissistic leaders; who succeeds and who fails, Harvard Business School Press, Boston, 2007

E. Maex – *Werken met Mindfulness; basisoefeningen*; about working with Mindfulness using basic exercises; Lannoo, Tielt, 2008

J. Melissen – *Diplomatie; Radarwerk van de internationale politiek* – about diplomacy as an instrument of international politics; Van Gorcum, Assen, 1999

L. Moratis – *Maatschappelijk Verantwoord Ondernemen; Basisboek MVO*; about Socially Responsible Business Practices, Koninklijke van Gorcum, Assen, 2006

Dr. I. Nuijten – Servant-Leadership; Paradox or Diamond in the Rough? A Multidimensional Measure and Empirical Evidence – doctoral thesis 2011

J. Nuttin; V. Hoorens – *Sociale beïnvloeding; toetsbaar leren over gedrag*; about social influencing and verifiable learning about behaviour, Leuven University Press, 2008

S. Piët – *Het Groot Communicatiedenkboek* - a new look into communication; Pearson Benelux, Amsterdam, 2005

R.E. Quinn – *Een kader voor managementvaardigheden*; a management briefing providing a framework for management skills; Academic Service, The Hague, 1998

R.E. Quinn – Building the bridge as you walk on it; a guide for leading change; John Wiley & Sons, Jossey-Bass, San Francisco, 2004

P.F. Rollin – 42 rules for your new leadership role, Super Star Press, California, 2011

W. Shadid – *Culturele diversiteit en interculturele communicatie; Verschenen in Veghel, H. van: Waarden onder de meetlat; Het Europese waardenonderzoek in discussie* – about cultural diversity and intercultural communication; Damon bv, Budel, 2002

Prof. Dr. L.U. de Sitter – *Synergetisch produceren; Human Resources Mobilisation in de productie; een inleiding in de structuurbouw*; Synergetic production, about HR Mobilisation in production, a managerial substantiation and methodology for integral redesign of production systems; Van Gorcum, Assen, 2000

W.L. Tiemeijer, C.A Thomas, H.M. Prast – *De menselijke beslisser; over de psychologie van keuze en gedrag* – about the psychology of choice and behaviour, Amsterdam University Press, Amsterdam, 2009

Max Weber on charisma and institution building; The University of Chicago Press, Chicago, 1968

European Journal of work and psychology; Volume 8, March 1999; Psychology Press ltd, East Sussex, UK

APPENDIX 2 BUILDING BLOCKS OF KEY LEADERSHIP FEATURES

KLF	BUILDING BLOCKS	EXPLANATION
Social features	Trustworthy	People trust you as a person for who you are, what you say and how you act.
	Interested	You are sincerely interested in other people. You are curious about their story and their motives, without making a value judgment.
	People-oriented	The person is important for you. In your actions, you think about the consequences this may have for others.
	Authentic	You do not play-act and you are trustworthy and credible. You are being yourself.
	Tact	You have the ability to assess what is appropriate in a certain situation. This may be orally and/or in writing. The timing of what you say, write and do comes as second nature to you.
	Empathy	You have the ability to put yourself in someone else's shoes and be understanding of his situation.
	Communicative skills	You say the right things at the right times, be it one-on-one or in a group. People like listening to you and you can listen to others in a way that no one else can.

KLF	BUILDING BLOCKS	EXPLANATION
Observed features	Calm	When others are busy or become emotional, you emanate calm, despite the fact that the adrenaline is flowing within you as well.
	Stress-resistant	Everybody may encounter stress, but you are perfectly capable of channeling it and you do not show it, despite time, pressure, and risks. The possible lack of internal room to maneuver that threatens to arise causes you to perform better.
	Obliging	Your inner discipline ensures that you look impeccable at all times. Apart from this, you are friendly, polite and helpful.
	Flair	You stand behind what you do and you emanate this. You present your message in a smart, open and charming manner, full of conviction.
	Charisma	You emanate power and self-assuredness without effort and without even noticing. What you radiate ensures that people follow you.
	Self-confidence	You trust in your abilities. It is this conviction and self-confidence that you display.

KLF	BUILDING BLOCKS	EXPLANATION
Action features	Tough	You can be unrelenting when necessary and, although you show an understanding of emotions, you do not allow emotions to lead you. You are strict in your assessment of the arguments.
	Demanding	You expect a lot from yourself and from others. You stretch the boundaries of possibility and remain critical at all times.
	Consistent	You are straightforward and people will not be surprised by the outcome of your decision. It is predictable.
	Proactive	You take the initiative before the situation requires. This way, you ensure that you keep hold of the reins.
	Decisive	You are swift and clear. You make firm decisions, without engaging in endless discussions
	Responsible	You do not hide behind the decisions of others. You take responsibility for your actions and your team's actions.
	Courage	You have the courage to take action. When others are in doubt because of the possible consequences, you dare to carry on.
	Ambition	You have an inner drive. You do your utmost to improve yourself and the organization. Boundaries are set by others.
	Vigor	You firmly transform ideas and thoughts into action.
	Resilience	You are determined to reach your goal, regardless of the setbacks you may encounter on the way.

KLF	BUILDING BLOCKS	EXPLANATION
Diplomatic features	Ethical	You are honest and sincere. You are always able to look at yourself in the mirror because you act in accordance with generally accepted values and standards.
	Exemplary	Your actions are impeccable. Others consider your behavior a good example.
	Articulate	You have the ability to apply the proper tone of voice and choice of words in order to clarify the topic of discussion or your opinion and to add substance to it.
	Etiquette	You know the generally accepted conventions of politeness, which you can apply properly under all circumstances. You have a feel for (informal) relations.
	Cultural awareness	You are aware of the different cultures in this world. You are able to adapt to other customs at a level that is acceptable for all parties.
	Negotiating skills	In negotiations, you respond to others in a capable, clever and targeted manner. After negotiations, both you and the other party feel that you have come to a fair agreement.

KLF	BUILDING BLOCKS	EXPLANATION
Guiding features	Adaptive	You are flexible in your attitude and actions. You adapt easily to organizations, persons and circumstances when required.
	Competitive	You have a healthy drive to perform better than others do.
	Inspirational	With your passion and enthusiasm, you are able to get people to follow, to encourage them and to push them to better performances than they would have thought possible.
	Team builder	You have the ability to create a team out of individuals. The team members are willing to work for each other and to prioritize the greater good.
	Persuasiveness	You have the power to persuade others. Your personal dominance, argumentation and tact enable you to get your opinion accepted or approved.
	Coaching skills	You are able to get maximum performance out of a group or individual by assuming various roles yourself (mentor, motivator, listener).
	Ability to delegate	You are able to transfer tasks and responsibilities to the right persons, enabling you to maintain more of an overview.
	Organizational capacity	You have a talent for organization, which enables you to successfully conclude projects in accordance with their conditions.

KLF	BUILDING BLOCKS	EXPLANATION
Mental features	Creative	You are original and inventive. You have no problem developing new ideas and you think outside of the box.
	Intelligent	You have the ability to see things in context, to quickly absorb learning material and to assess situations properly. You are able to quickly and effectively approach information and transform this into words and actions.
	Curious	You are extremely inquisitive by nature. As a general rule, you have more questions than answers and you are eager to learn.
	Self-knowledge	You know your strengths and lesser strengths. You know what you want and you know your boundaries. As a result of this, you are resilient when necessary. You also know exactly when to listen to your gut.
	Judge of character	You have insight into the driving forces and competences of other people and you are able to value them for what they are worth.
	Disciplined	You do what needs to be done, regardless of your mental and physical condition.
	Vision	You have realistic, long-term foresight about where you wish to go and how to get there.
	Sense of perspective	When the chips are down or people get bogged down in too much detail, you see the situation in perspective and you are able to pass this on to others.
	Analytical capacity	You are able to distinguish between major and minor issues. You find creative solutions and can break big problems into bite-size chunks. As such, you are able to set the priorities.
	Know-how	When you take part in discussions you can substantiate your opinions with facts.
	Situational awareness	You maintain perspective at all times and do not get bogged down in details. You are able to use a helicopter view independently and to evaluate factors of time, place and environment properly.